C000078336

PAULINE DANIELS
MY STORY

PAULINE DANIELS
MY STORY

*Stand Up And
Be Counted*

TrinityMirror Media

My, oh my.
This is for the four people who
have shaped my life and
loved me unconditionally.
My wonderful Nan, Doris.
My dear dear dad, Copper.
My lovely mum, Doreen.
And (wait for applause) the jewel
in the crown, my girl, Sarah . . .
Thank you x

PAULINE DANIELS

Stand Up And Be Counted

Editor: Peter Grant
Assistant Editors: Vicky Andrews, James Cleary
Design: Zoe Bevan
Liverpool Daily Post & Echo Archive: Brian Johnston
Additional Research: Cathy Roberts
Cover Photograph: Jim Connolly
Publicity Shots: Ricky McCabe
Other images courtesy of Liverpool Daily Post and ECHO,
Pauline Daniels' private collection, Liverpool Playhouse,
Royal Court Liverpool and Granada TV.

Copyright text: Trinity Mirror / Pauline Daniels
Published in Great Britain in hardback form in 2011
Published and produced by: Trinity Mirror Media,
PO Box 48, Old Hall Street, Liverpool L69 3EB

TrinityMirror Media

Business Development Director: Mark Dickinson
Executive Editor: Ken Rogers
Senior Editor: Steve Hanrahan
Editor: Paul Dove
Senior Art Editor: Rick Cooke
Trinity Mirror Media Marketing Executive: Claire Brown
Sales and Marketing Manager: Elizabeth Morgan
Sales and Marketing Assistant: Karen Cadman

Printed by CPI Mackay

ISBN: 9781906802745

PAULINE DANIELS
MY STORY

CONTENTS

A Joyous Performer

"This lady belts out a stream
of observations about the
things in life that make
everyone laugh."

WHEN Pauline Daniels stands alone on stage and tells jokes, gags and sketches the men laugh and nod – but it is the girls she is really talking to.

Once described as "five feet two inches tall and half as heavy as the Liver Building," she broke into a male-dominated industry – the tough world of stand-up performance.

This feisty, strawberry blonde progressed from the citadel of working men's clubs to holiday camps; radio and TV programmes galore.

And from there she triumphed in West End musicals at The London Palladium and also thesping in 'Shirley Valentine' and other histrionic dramas.

La Daniels' husky voice was nurtured on Birkenhead breezes, Wirral shrimps and little drops of tickle tonic. It is fine-tuned to any climate – in any part of the country. Pauline's humour travels well.

This lady delivers a stream of observations about the things in life that make everyone laugh.

Men are often the target – is it revenge for all the mother-in-law jokes she heard growing up? She soon reduces the macho men in the audience to wimps.

Her topics range from all the experiences of her wonderful life – so many odd years. And, according to her, they have been very odd years.

Marriage, supermarkets, holidays, mobile phones, running her own theatre and, of course, her trademark – the battleground of her struggle with the male species – until she stopped struggling.

Pauline has stamped her own unique mark on her comedy career, saying: "I am all woman and I have a big girl's voice and you are going to sit there and listen and laugh."

She became the first comedienne to appear on Granada TV's hit series 'The Comedians'.

Pauline is still loving her showbusiness life and if she doesn't get any laughs from her comedy, she can always rely on her singing – exercising those glorious lungs.

Miss Daniels is a truly wonderful, versatile, joyous performer.

KEN DODD
OBE

Showtime

"Five minutes to curtain,
Miss Daniels..."

ANOTHER dressing room, another show. From Shirley Valentine to panto, I've been there and done that.

And I will carry on doing that. Whether a musical or a straight play, or my beloved stand up. I am here to stand up and be counted.

I wouldn't have it any other way.

Now, in my 50s, and three husbands later, I am celebrating 30 years in showbusiness as an actress, comedian, singer and theatre-manager.

Not a bad CV for a 'rag arse' from Birkenhead.

I can't juggle though. Ask my bank manager and he will tell you that. I attempt to, but without much success. All balls in the air, eh girls?

I hope that you enjoy following me on every stage I've been on. Shakespeare said: "All the world's a stage," and it is. I am well read you know – I have an Honorary Fellowship from Liverpool John Moores University. Hey, who would have thought it?

But I am what I am (not Shirley Bassey – I'm not on her money anyway). In this book I'll take you with me through the world of the working men's clubs, cruises, panto, husbands, theatre, telly, entertaining Her Majesty's troops, more husbands, holiday camps.

All the ups and downs, and even the odd conflict with a bunch of nuns. A very bad habit to get into . . .

Sometimes it has been a lonely life, but never, ever, dull or miserable.

I compare it to a creative boxing or wrestling match – a woman competing in a man's world, but always surrounded by the love of a wonderful family and a few very dear friends.

I am sure it's all been to make me a better person.

I started my career in the working men's clubs all over the country in 1980 as a female comic. It was no picnic. There were wasps though – there always are at picnics.

I was, I now think, hated by the male comics because I used to sing and then do a few gags and I was loathed by the girl singers because I got more money than they did. My career took off when I picked up where the 'old school' comics left off.

When things became politically correct and people STOPPED doing sexist jokes, that's when I found the gap in the market – it was the best time to START.

After all, we girls who became women had listened to those male comics for so many years, slagging off their wives and their mother-in-laws.

I was once told by a television company that I couldn't do a mother-in-law joke because it was, "someone's nan" and it wouldn't seem right.

Relatively speaking, that's enough to make you scream. It made me scream . . . with laughter. The gloves were on.

It was a man, of course, who said this, and although I didn't do the particular joke, I've never forgotten his reasoning.

It makes things clearer to me about why women have always found it harder to break into comedy – because it's not only dominated by men, but most of the TV companies are run by men, too.

Still, I feel as though I've happily got my own back on any man who has upset me personally and professionally. I always attract female audiences (for obvious reasons because of my material) and as strange as it may seem, whenever the men LAUGH, I honestly think that they are oblivious to the fact that they are laughing at THEMSELVES!

I totally agree with the philosophy in the famous book and its adage that Women are from Venus and Men are from Mars and, thank God – after all is said and done – I LOVE MEN.

I wouldn't sleep with anything else. Well, apart from that camel once, but that was a totally drunken accident.

I just thought it was a bloke with his tie caught in his zip causing his back to look as though it had a hump.

Ugly experience.

Drink can certainly get you into a mess. At a celebrity party I was asked by a major regional paper if I would pose naked for a charity appeal. Being quite well oiled, I said: "Yesshh!"

I forgot all about it until they rang and said that the photographer was on her way . . . Oops, I've done it again (sorry, Britney).

It was all for a good cause. I did it for The Lily Centre Breast Cancer Support Group of which I am a patron and, at least, it was a lady photographer.

The one thing I (sort of) forgot to do was mention it to my daughter, Sarah, who was working at the same paper. I did the photo shoot, with a newspaper and a gigantic feather boa covering my modesty and that was that.

Until the morning of Christmas Eve when Sarah rang me and said: "I went to the work Christmas do on

Saturday, Mum, and all sorts of people kept coming up to me and were asking how old you were. I told them you were 112."

Good gag, Sarah.

My daughter then told them the truth that I was 50 and she reported back that they were all saying how great I looked for my age. Cheek.

I didn't think much about it until after about the fourth time, and then I asked: "Why, Sarah?"

And she said: "Haven't you seen the naked pictures of you, Mum?"

I shook my head open-mouthed. I said: "Oh love, I'm sorry, only it was for charity and . . ."

"No, it's fine," she said.

"They are lovely photos and they are in the paper tonight."

Phew . . . you see, you never stop embarrassing your kids.

Actually, I was quite proud of those photos, not bad at all, even though I say so myself.

Sitting here now, looking at myself in the make-up glass, I think: "You really do know when you're getting old – don't you, girl?"

And then I talk to the wall. Isn't that right,wall?

I'm still waiting for tights. I know that seems a bit of a random thing to say but I am random. As I write this, it's now the interval on the third day in a run of a panto and I am still waiting for tights. Black ones.

I've got normal ones but that's not the point. At least my shoes arrived today which is a God send. I am at the age when the dreaded bunions rear their ugly heads

17

and I have a beauty on my left foot. Nothing major on the right, funny that? On first discovering my bunion, I rang my Mum for that sympathy that we know only mums can give: "Mum, I've got a bunion."

"Serves you right," she said. "I warned you about those awful platform shoes when you were young."

You know what's happening when you look in the mirror and your mother is looking back at you. I've never been a beauty. In fact, I always used to stand in front of the mirror and ask my mum: "Why am I so ugly?"

But although I wasn't the prettiest apple I always had a great sense of humour, and although it can be intimidating to men, it can also attract them. Honest.

I have had my fair share of boyfriends over the years and 'secret' admirers.

I can say that because none of us will ever know if that's true (but it is . . . I was there).

In 1913 I would have been a suffragette and probably imprisoned, but for now I can get on with my story.

The great times I have had, the hard times too.

And the downright sh** ones (I will kill this book editor for putting asterisks in).

I know I will be skipping all over the place but that is sort of how I work. I am a stand up – it happens. I can start a story then go off on a tangent, but always come back to the original story.

I'm a bit like that when I do housework. I start the job and then think "stuff this" and then piss off out to do some shopping!

I am a self-confessed shopaholic. I have kept QVC

in business single handedly for the last 18 years. The trouble, is I have the expensive taste for such shops as Gucci, Prada and YSL but have the budget for Primani and Matt Allen, OK . . . Primark and Matalan.

I love new technology as well, but then I must be the first woman who went out 29 years ago for a loaf of bread and came back with an Amstrad computer.

Now, with Twitter and Facebook, people know more about me than I do. I have terrible trouble, 'ganning' – spilling the beans . . . talking too much. You get the picture.

When I was working on the radio, I told everyone EVERYTHING. Savage memories.

Please enjoy this book and know that – hand on my heart – for all the pitfalls and the mistakes and the misery . . . yes, I really would do it ALL again.

Now the book.

It's showtime . . .

CHAPTER I

Relatively Speaking

"I probably get my balls from my mum. And my nan. I definitely get my sense of humour from my dad. He was daft."

DOREEN and Charlie grew up on the opposite sides of the tracks. Mum in Higher Tranmere – she insists on the "higher" because it distinguished you from "Donkey Town", which was how some people described Lower Tranmere.

Mum, you weren't half a snob.

While she was being a little princess, Charles Malam, one of eight lads, was being a nuisance in the North End of Birkenhead. No arse in his trousers and velvet sleeves so you could wipe your nose.

I have to laugh. Dad had no airs and graces. He used to fight over what they called, "the Bobby's clothes".

Apparently, a bundle of clothes donated to those children who were in need by the police.

Here was a man who used to steal an onion – yes, an onion – on the way to school every morning.

His mum was behind him one day and she 'shopped him' to the woman who owned the fruit and veg stall. The woman already knew, and if it had been an apple or a banana she would have told the police, but it was only an onion – and he used to eat it like an apple.

He always knew his onions though.

Dad was smoking from a very early age and one day when he was outside the pictures, having a sly ciggie, he spotted his mum and sister-in-law coming toward him. He put the cigarette in the pocket of his new trousers . . . lit. When nan and Gertie got to him there was a blaze of smoke coming from his kecks pocket, but he refused to admit he had been smoking.

Liar, liar, your pants on fire – that must be when the phrase was coined.

When I think about Doreen and "Copper", as my dad was called, there really wasn't any way these two should have ever met and married but they did. They had a nice courtship.

It seems they spent a lot of time at the pictures and in a milk bar in Grange Road called Oliveries, owned by a lovely Italian couple, who opened a couple of milk bars in Birkenhead.

Mum and dad then both worked on the buses together when they got married.

Doreen was Copper's 'clippy' (the bus conductor), which in theory sounds good. The only trouble was, whenever they had a row, Doreen either would, or wouldn't ring the bell. This got Copper in trouble because they would fly past loaded bus stops, leaving angry would-be passengers waving their fists and other things at his bus.

She also had quite a nice trick up her sleeve. On Copper's day off she would roll over in bed and whisper in his ear: "Would you go and start my shift and I'll be in soon?"

Of course, Copper would go off and do this, but Doreen would be nowhere to be seen, taking two days off. She was only getting him back for the "name" thing . . . honest.

Their wedding was as traditional as it could be.

March 25, 1950, was still a time when the nation was suffering from the backlash of the war and it was still hard to get certain things.

In fact, they had a cake that collapsed, as it was just a little short on certain ingredients, and there wasn't a big white frock. But then Copper only had 7s 6p in his pocket on the day he got married, so times were fairly hard.

Doreen's Auntie Beryl was her maid of honour. She was also her best friend.

Beryl was three months younger than Doreen and they were almost brought up together and went everywhere together. Copper had to take Beryl everywhere.

Sadly we lost Beryl in 2009, but I have a strong feeling that she never, ever forgave dad for pinching her mate.

Doreen, was now called "Two Soups Soprano". She had a bad back and whenever she carried teas in from the kitchen she just looked like Julie Walters in the 'Two Soups' sketch on Victoria Wood's television show.

The 'Soprano' part – well make up your own mind.

Doreen was the eldest of two children. Albert was her younger brother and Doris, her mum, was widowed at the age of 36. Doreen's dad had died in Tunisia during the war.

I never met granddad George, but very strange things occur to me, all connected to him.

I was once told by a medium that George was with me. Strangely, I haven't felt his presence since nan died. I like to think he has enough to do looking after her.

Doreen's childhood was a very happy one before her dad went away to war. He was a bit of a right one was our George and it was a regular thing for him to come home from the pub, along with every waif and stray of the day, who he had taken under his wing.

He would take them into the cellar, where there was a piano and a boxing ring.

These men ate whatever Doris had rustled up for them and then knocked seven kinds of shit out of each other, while some drunk played the piano.

There was always music and laughter in the house and when George went away to war life changed drastically.

Albert was a sickly child and if anyone ever picked on him Doreen would punch their lights out. They were separated when they were evacuated and Albert wasn't in the best of homes.

Mum wasn't happy where she was but the spinster who was looking after her wasn't a bad lady. When Doris heard about her unhappy kids she went straight to Wales – packed their stuff and brought them home.

Mum always had to look after her little brother and she had a reputation of knocking lads out left, right and centre. She was quite a tubby kid so she had to stick up for herself.

"Soprano . . . "

I probably get my balls from my mum. And my nan. I definitely get my sense of humour from my dad. He was daft.

This seems to be a perfect place to tell you a really funny story told to me by a woman in The Springfield – a fabulous hotel cabaret venue as it was. I was stood at the bar and she said that she had a true story to tell me. They really always are the best ones.

It seems that during the war there was a man whose job it was to visit homes and distribute gas masks. However, he was only supposed to give them out to those he could actually see at the time. This woman said that they were quite a big family and her eldest sister, Francis, was out.

The guy came and gave them all their masks and when her mum said to him: "What about our Fanny's?" he replied with typical Scouse speed: "Sorry love, we only cater for your faces".

This was all before I made my debut on this earth and remained the only child of Doreen and Copper. I have been spoilt by both of them for the last 50 odd years.

My dad, in particular, wouldn't let the wind blow on me.

Charlie Malam ran up the stairs of St Catherine's Hospital in Tranmere to be told by Sadie, a cleaner on the ward, that: "Yours is the red head in the end bed."

Anyway, that was how I was introduced for the first time onto the big stage. Bigger stages were to follow.

I was a fairly good child I think. Well, no . . . I was a credit to my mum and dad and they were always proud of me. I loved school but it didn't always love me.

I used to do impressions of teachers and, yes, I was caught a couple of times – but I was the class clown and so when anything went wrong, I always seemed to get the blame.

On one occasion my mum received a letter from the school stating that I was seen on the top deck of the number 60 bus going down Whetstone Lane smoking.

My mum was straight down to the school, because on the date they said I was doing this dreadful thing, as luck would have it, I was actually out with her at the Little Theatre in Grange Road West – so it couldn't have been ME. (Pause for applause).

Mum and I did the theatre experience. Dad didn't really like the theatre. She took me to the Empire to see Frankie Vaughan and Jimmy Tarbuck. We were in the queue and Tarbuck passed by. He rubbed my head and said: "Hello, Ginger, what's your name?"

I said: "Pauline", and he told me his wife was called Pauline, too. I'd like to see him rub my head and call me ginger NOW.

The best show my mum ever took me to was at the Plaza in Birkenhead.

I was nine and absolutely adored my music – any music – but definitely Rock and Roll. The one and only Little Richard was on with a host of stars including Rory Storm and the Hurricanes, complete with Richard Starkey as their drummer.

I'd met him before. In fact, Ringo and I were bosom pals. In 1961 I was on holiday at Butlin's Pwllheli along with Rory's drummer, who was there for the summer season.

I was too young to dance so I used to look after the handbags and sit by Ringo. We became quite matey. I must remind him if I ever bump into him in one of his mansions.

Last time I saw him was when he had a right go at his home town on the BBC's Jonathan Ross show.

When asked if he had missed anything about the place, he cockily said "NO."

This was after being paid a fortune for appearing on the roof of St George's Hall for the opening of Capital of Culture in 2008. He was plugging his album about the place he grew up in: Liverpool.

"Liverpool I Never Let You Down," he said.

Peace and love, Ringo . . . Peace and love.

Anyway, I never smoked on that bus, honest.

Back in school, I was the kid who instantly had the blackboard rubber thrown at her. Teachers never even looked – they just assumed. It took me four years to make a cookery apron in needlework.

I really only left school with a completed pump bag, which was never of any use as I hated sports.

One day my 'best friends' Barbara and Andrea actually hung me on the hook in the changing room loo.

On the few occasions I was found by the gym teacher, I went out on the hockey field and tried to take out as many people with the hockey stick as I could. I was always sent off. We had a few 'incidents' at Prenton Secondary School. We had one girl come to us from Park High School because she had been expelled for being pregnant.

I wouldn't mind, but she had already been expelled a year before from Birkenhead High School for being pregnant so she was popping 'em out all over the place, sliding down the educational ladder whilst doing so. It was a shame because she was really clever.

I remember she had lovely handwriting, which is obviously no use when you're lying on your back with your legs in the air, but you'd have thought with her intelligence she'd have learnt her lesson after the first baby.

I think she went on to have quite a few kids. She married the guilty penis though, and as far as I am aware they were living quite happily in a shoe somewhere.

There was no chance of me ever getting pregnant. Well, only Quasimodo would have fancied me. I was a little tub with ginger hair and glasses. Actually I'm the same today – except for the hair. That's out of a bottle.

Teachers at Prenton were alright, I suppose. There was a lovely one, Mrs Shuttleworth, who, unfortunately, was very timid and couldn't keep the class together. She taught French, but by this time I was quite bored with 'Le Language' because Mr Hooper at Mersey Park had taught us all since we were seven.

At the age of 11, I was sitting there waiting for everyone else to play catch-up.

As soon as I could escape French I chose History and loved it, as well as English, Drama and Music.

I even won a prize: The Junior Speech and Drama Prize. Now, for anyone who knows me, they would never believe that – but it's true.

Music was a hoot. I was the only kid taking O Level music. I would have two-hour periods on my own with a lovely, but none-the-less quite batty teacher. When she couldn't think of anything for me to do she would tell me to tidy up the record collection, while she disappeared to a place I know not, probably just a simple case of the staff room for a fag.

I would put Chopin on the player and tidy up the rest whilst Andrea and Barbara would be outside the window just simply taking the proverbial piss.

I didn't stay on to finish my O Levels. I got a job in Cranes Music Store and left. Mum always said that if I got a job I could leave. I went along to that interview and there were two women in the sheet music department:

one little old fussy blonde and the other – I can't really be sure that it was a woman to be honest. She was a bit scary and looked as though she was a hooker at weekends – with the St Helens rugby league team!

Isn't it funny how it really is a small world? My nan used to clean for the Cranes Store – she used to take me with her when I was on school holidays. They had millions of pianos (okay, about three pianos, but it seemed like a piano in every room to me).

I do believe that childhood shapes your later life.

I had an extremely happy and contented childhood. I didn't mind being an only child. In fact, it was great.

Being an only child meant I didn't have to share my lovely mum and dad with anyone else. I would have loved to have gone to university, though.

I got there in the end, though but not by three years of studying. I did all mine along the way. I love learning. I learn something every single day. I would have enjoyed the whole university student life . . . especially the social side.

Friendship is very important to me, and I have realised just lately how loyal and true my friends are – they are there when I need them. I know I am there for them.

My best mate is my old bass player, Colin, but I have a lot of good close friends who I adore. We all need that.

Looking back to my post-school, pre-job years, it all comes tumbling back. For instance, I started smoking when I was 13 – and I don't know why. I suppose I thought it was a very grown up thing to do. All the best movie stars smoked, everyone on telly lit up a fag. Most of my family smoked – it seemed the natural thing to do.

I gave up smoking in 2009 and was doing well. Then, when my dad died, my world fell apart and I reached for the ciggies again. At this moment in time I am always ready for a new start and I am giving up again (see volume 2!).

I've made my mind up. I've seen a beautiful handbag and coat that I could afford if I stopped. I intend to spend all other non-smoking savings on travel to New York, Paris and Rome next year and I will wear my new coat and carry my new handbag.

See I told you I ramble.

Back to school . . .

I had a pretty normal childhood, my mum worked so my lovely nan brought me up and I suppose I became very grown up at an early age because nan never treated me as a child . . . she always spoke to me as an adult. I learned a lot from our Doris, God bless her.

If I could go back to my teenage years I'd be a punk . . . I missed out on all of that because I married and became a mum far too young

I feel guilty about everything! I really should have been a Catholic. I blame myself for everything, such as all my relationships going wrong. I always think it's MY fault. I know it isn't, but I believe I might be to blame for some of the awful world disasters we've had. Guilt.

People say, 'Pauline, you don't suffer fools gladly'. I don't suffer fools at all. I get that from my mum – a strong woman, a born-leader and a bossy bugger. I'm just the same!

From leaving school to having my lovely daughter, Sarah, was a really upbeat time. I had loads of different jobs, made a few really close friends, some okay boyfriends and then when I met Dave (hubby 1) I just laughed all the time. I had a great time.

As I mentioned, my first job after I left school was in Cranes music shop. I loved the whole experience. I worked in the sheet music department with two rather eccentric women and it's funny how life changes.

There was a little office at the side of the counter and I remember it as if it was yesterday. They both smoked Consulate menthol cigarettes, and they would take it in turns to nip off round the side for a fag.

I was smoking No 6 at the time and I just remember thinking how very sophisticated these two rather odd women looked with these long, pure white cigarettes, so I decided it was for ME. Besides, they were menthol, so probably healthy!

I loved the way the local "stars" used to come in and buy their sheet music. Pete Price, who is now one of our number one radio presenters on Radio City, was the host of The Shakespeare club at that time.

He used to come in wearing his now famous "hot pants" and a full length fur coat. He always had the most gigantic smokey quartz ring on his finger, and I was mesmerised.

Years later I worked in panto with Pete, and he came in one day to say he had been to the jewellers. He was thinking of selling a ring, and he took out the ring . . . and it was MY ring, the one I had fantasised about for years. I had always looked longingly at the ring and I used to say that, one day, I would have a ring like that. Now, here it was, staring me in the face.

I tried it on and just like Cinderella, it fitted. I told him the story and he said that if he was going to sell it in the future, he would give me first refusal – I so want that ring!

We had many stars working in the city who popped into the shop. We also had this awful little man who was in charge of pianos and guitars who was obnoxious to everyone, despite who they were.

One day Manitas de Platas, probably one of the most famous Spanish guitarists ever, wandered in. He had a problem with his own guitar and was working at the Philharmonic Hall that night and needed a replacement.

He took a guitar from the wall and proceeded to play the most beautiful piece of music.

However, this horrid little man screamed at him to put the guitar back on the wall. He had no idea who HE was – not really good if you are supposed to know your guitars.

The man with him tried to explain to him that he needed to buy a couple of replacement guitars and told him exactly who he was. No matter – he just shouted louder that he didn't care. With that Manitas de Platas buggered off to Rushworths in Whitechapel.

When I left Cranes I went to work for a car showroom in the office. I did the accounts – God knows how. I knew nothing about accounts and once I'd run out of fingers and toes, my maths were knackered.

I always seem to blag my way into jobs. Well, my logic seemed to be right: if you get a job, pound to a penny, someone will show you the ropes and it worked for many a job. And I had many.

I got bored pretty quickly and in the early 70s you could walk out of one job on a Friday and start a new one the following Monday. My logic never let me down until I got a job as a telex operator for an assay office, where they'd test the purity of metals.

I bulls****ed my way through the interview and then, when I got the offer, I turned up on the Monday morning, only to be locked in a room on my own with this monster of a machine. I couldn't make head nor tail of.

I will not be beaten by a machine, and by lunch time I was chatting with a brand new friend in Peru.

I took a job once on the Dock Road in Birkenhead on reception. All I could see all day was Flour Mill Wagons, back and forth from Spillers. I lasted a week.

I flitted all over the place.

I worked for a hospital in the accounts office, a chartered surveyors on the reception, a travel agents. I even worked in pubs. By the way, that was by far MY favourite job. Well, it was sociable and I didn't have to get up early . . . perfect.

I hated going to work. When I started to do the clubs it was the best thing that had ever happened to me. I loved it from day one, and I love my working life even more today. Every day is different and every day is a challenge. If I didn't have work – that means, I'm meeting myself coming back most days – I think I would just curl up and die.

I could never retire. I just want to go the same way as

Tommy Cooper and Eric Morecambe. It would be the perfect end to a perfect working life.

It's sad my love life hasn't been as good – if it had, I'd still probably want to die "on the job".

Now where was I . . .

TOP 10 ADVICE FOR THE YOUNGER GENERATION

1. LISTEN . . . To your mother.
Sorry girls, but she is always right.

2. AIM . . . For your goal
and don't stop until you score.

3. DON'T . . . Get married young.
Or just don't get married – it's a piece of paper
that sometimes ruins a good relationship.

4. HAVE . . . Loads of gay friends.
They are better to take shopping than girls.
And they tell the truth.

5. AVOID . . . Being a grandmother.
At least before you're 30.

6. GET . . . A dog.
They are more faithful than men.

7. RESPECT . . . Your elders.
You will be one, one day.

8. AT 70 . . . Do something you never did when you were younger. I'm going to dye my hair purple.

9. NEVER . . . Take drugs.

10. LOVE YOU . . . You can't love and respect, or love anyone else until YOU do.

CHAPTER 2

Women Are From Salons, Men Are From Garages

"Once a month, every normal, living, breathing woman becomes a bloody monster. The only positive thing is you can get off with a shoplifting charge."

AT the age of 18 I was married to husband number one. At 19, I had given birth to Sarah – my one and only child. I did it once, and I didn't like it.

I was in the maternity hospital in Wallasey, watching the most ridiculous Maltesers advert on the telly where a guy slid along the aisle in a supermarket and got covered in chocolate. I had seen this commercial a million times before, and it had never had an effect on me at all, but this night I started to laugh . . . and laugh . . . and laugh and then . . . oops.

I had no idea what the hell was happening to me, but I knew that I was very bloody wet. . . my waters had broken. I jumped off the bed and shouted for the nurse. She was then following me around the ward with a mop and bucket saying: "For God's sake, Pauline, stand bloody still will you!"

I replied: "But I want a wee."

"Just bloody do it for God's sake, it's not going to make a bit of difference to me."

The next morning at 5am the pains started. When I was in labour with Sarah I was lying in my bed in hospital smoking like a chimney, while some maintenance man was drilling the metal bars that went around the beds with the curtains on. Thanks to health and safety at work, you just can't have that kind of fun these days.

Oh, how things have changed. I go to visit people in hospital now and outside there are legions of people in their pyjamas puffing away on ciggies.

Actually, there are so many young girls who wear their pyjamas to go out these days, you're not sure whether they are patients or not.

Anyway, after 12 hours of labour, at 5pm my beautiful daughter was born. There and then I decided . . . never again.

Now, there were many things that I could do to stop this ever happening again:

1) THE PILL

I had tried that before and it was a very effective contraceptive because I put three stone on and no one wanted to 'give me one.'

2) THE DUTCH CAP

I was worried that it may be a little tight and not fit round my head (I'm joking, but leave it in . . . the book that is). I'd heard all about the cap. At times of great passion you have to insert this thing which usually flies off the end of your fingers and buggers off out of the window. I now believe that's what all those UFOs were that were spotted a few years ago.

3) THE COIL

Oh, the dreaded coil. If any man wants to know what it's like to have a coil fitted, I suggest they go find an umbrella, shove it up their arse and open the bugger out. It bloody hurts. On the plus side – if you stand with one leg on the telly and one out of the window you will get the best Channel Five reception in your street.

I opted for the safest method . . .

4) A VASECTOMY

For him. Great, now he was just like the Christmas tree – his balls were just for decoration.

I wonder about men's balls. I mean, when they become old, they just turn into a sack for them to sit on. That's another thing I've always wondered about: why is it that every man, no matter how handsome he is, turns into Goofy when he's having an orgasm?

It's been a constant form of entertainment all my life and better if he's on top. Well, it has to be that way now, because no woman over the age of 40 should ever get on top. Everything droops far too much.

Sarah was beautiful when she was born (and still is). She wasn't all crinkly and red like babies I'd seen before. Her skin was like peaches and cream and I was a wife and a mum. End of life as I knew it, I thought.

Everything would change from that day on and although it seemed my dreams were never going to come true, I knew that whatever else happened, this little bundle was going to be whatever she wanted to be, and I was going to help in every single way I could.

Life isn't fair when it comes to doling out the things that happen to the sexes.

For instance, what happens to a man during puberty? His voice goes deeper; his balls hit his knees and he makes friends with his wrist – a habit that some never grow out of. They do it in the pictures. I wish they'd stop using my hand, though.

But what happens to women?

Well, Mother Nature – whom I don't think is at all fair – strikes a woman down with something called a menstrual cycle (and that's not a Japanese motor bike, by the way).

When she hits us with it she delivers a totally irrational person into the home. Once a month, every normal, living, breathing woman becomes a bloody monster.

The only positive thing is you can get off with a shop-lifting charge – but everything else that comes with it is a nightmare.

Mother Nature hits us with all of what I call s***. (C'mon get rid of the asterisks, this is a grown-up book.)

Basically, she's handing us countless alibis on a plate should we ever need to take revenge on the male sex who, in my grounded way, I believe causes all our problems in the first place.

It seems only fair when you consider that every 28 days an unwelcome character from the film 'The Exorcist' arrives in your kitchen.

Which wouldn't be so bad except for all the contraptions that go along with this massive change that happens to our bodies. Whatever happened to Dr White?

If you are over 45 you'll remember him. He was responsible for us women wearing a very strange belt that went round our waists with two hooks – front and back – that attached to his prototype 'Pamper' really. That's how I remember it.

There are women under 40 squirming now at the thought. Yeah, well, we lived with it.

It was a new meaning to the phrase "being Pampered."

Then there was always the alternative. The tampon.

Pause for dramatic music here please, publishers.

Well, it transpired that these could give you . . . 'toxic shock syndrome.' Toxic riots more like. I have carried one in my handbag for years knowing that should I ever be attacked by a strange man, I could get it out and shove it up his nose – that'll sort him!

Tampons come in different absorbency levels.

Be careful, girls, I used one on holiday once, dived into the pool and the whole pool disappeared.

I was on water tablets for two years after that.

Then came 'Wings'. What an innovative thing they are, very hygenic. You just drop your knickers and they fly into the bin on their own. Oh, if only.

The worst thing about these little swines is that they have an adhesive strip and if you are not paying attention you could quite easily give yourself a quick impromptu bikini wax.

Now that's something men don't have to do. I would love to have been a fly-on-the-wall in those beauty salons when these lads today have what is affectionately known as a 'back, sack and crack.'

It's something I would VOLUNTEER to do as a job. It would hold great satisfaction for me. Of course, I would be picturing different people on the table and, oh yes, two of them would be previous husbands.

Once the puberty thing happens to the lads, it's over, but we girls have to put up with our 'monthly visitors' for a good 30 to 40 years. I started my periods at a very early age. I was in school and literally thought I was bleeding to death.

My mate, who I told behind the bike sheds (even though we didn't have bike sheds), informed me what it was and the teacher later 'sorted' me out.

I want to get this off my chest, too. I was 10 when I started to wear a bra. It was a really silky thing and when I came home from school and took my tie off, there was the bloody thing hanging round my neck. It had slipped up throughout the day.

I was devastated when I discovered pubic hair. I really thought I was a child of the devil, so I did what I thought was right. I cut it off . . . and put it in a plastic bag. I don't know what I was thinking. Maybe when I found out it was normal, I should have stuck it back on? If that was possible I'd be okay today.

Ask yourself: why do you stop growing hair where you should have it and start growing it where you shouldn't? I own a single hair epilator. Please explain to me why we get just one coarse hair that sticks out on our face and feels enormous, and how come we go straight to it. It's like we have a radar for them.

Oh, growing up and getting older is s***!

(I see, asterisks again.)

Then something delightful hits called 'The Menopause' or "the change", as elderly women like to call it and they only 'MOUTH' the words for fear of (God only knows), what.

The Menopause hits us both differently, too. He grows his hair, buys a sports car (usually red) or a motor bike and kicks his wife out in favour of a younger model.

We have problems we have no control over, such as mood swings, painful periods, night sweats, hot flushes and then we get to go regularly to have our breasts trapped in a vice.

When it first happened to me I went to the doctor and he did the usual blood test.

Then, I went for the results. He said that if I had murdered anyone in the last six months he was pretty confident he could get me off with it. My hormones were all over the place.

Some played the Glasgow Empire.

My hubby Kenny had only just found this "soul mate" and then this Menopause happened.

God bless him, it was so hot at night in the winter I would be naked with all the covers thrown off me and the windows wide open. He, unfortunately, had to sleep fully-clothed with his overcoat on.

You see, some men are prepared to go through all of these eventualities with you. A lesser man would have grown his hair, actually bought that red sports car and traded me in.

It's comforting to know that now I have other things to look forward to, but I hope that we sort of equal out in later life.

I have arthritis to embrace, but at least I have that lovely little HRT pill to help me through.

When the doctor first told me I needed HRT I thought it meant Husband Replacement Therapy.

I had a ball for months.

Oh, I have just been for my regular mammogram and I've realized exactly what it's like. If you want to prepare yourselves for it, girls, just take your bra off, which might be good. When I do that, quite a lot of wrinkles fall out of my face now.

Anyway here's my advice: take it off, go to your fridge, put one breast inside the fridge then slam the door – yep that feels exactly the same as what I have had done.

However uncomfortable, it's imperative that you go and do it regularly. While I was there at one session,

I was sat next to a woman. We were both dressed in those lovely fetching back-less gowns that the hospital give you, and I was reading a book. She spoke to me and said: "I've been waiting here for over a bloody hour."

I looked at her and, I'm sorry, but I was now facing a woman whose moustache would have challenged Tom Selleck in his Magnum days.

I was angry with her because she was moaning to the nurse about having to come back on the Saturday and was threatening not to keep her appointment. I have seen what breast cancer does and anyone who moans doesn't deserve the service, in my opinion. I am grateful that I am fair-haired though – I couldn't have coped with a moustache like hers.

Do modern women have any positive role models? Cheryl Cole beats women up, gets her image back on track, is loved by the nation, then splits from a two-timing dog. So far so good, we all love her, and now, she's thinking of going back to the cheat – some girls never learn.

Rihanna the same scenario: allegedly gets beaten up by her boyfriend, and then apparently gets back in contact with him.

Take a leaf out of Liz Taylor's book if you are going to fight with a man – be like her. She stood her ground, gave as good as she got and always ended up with a beautiful diamond for her trouble.

WAGs are not to be admired – they are to be pitied. They have very little sense, and far too much money. I sat next to one once at the theatre and when she wasn't talking to her mate she was sending texts on her phone. Later, when I got home, I was watching the football and lo and behold there was a very tall professional footballer on the bench answering the bloody thing – oops, you probably know who it was now.

Amy Winehouse: wasted talent, bad choice of men and drink and drugs, what a tragic loss – but her music lives on.

As far as I'm concerned, Kate Moss is a BAD advert for the female body.

So is Victoria Beckham, a so-called 'style icon' who is painfully skinny and wears shoes two sizes too big because of her bunions. That's not stylish, although she must be quite clever to have been able to hang on to David after all this time, and she is a tryer – she has made a career out of having no talent . . . now that's an art.

Talking about having no talent, I once had the misfortune to work on a show that was hosted by Jodie Marsh, who was so up her own arse it was unbelievable. She was co-hosting and kept coming into my dressing room to use the mirror, never knocked or asked, just walked in. After the third time I told her in a not-so -nice way to use her own bloody mirror and then, at the end of my spot, I thanked the other hostess . . . Jordan. She was fuming – RESULT.

There are a few that I do think deserve a mention like Victoria Wood, a very clever, hard working brilliant writer and performer, a woman to be admired and proud of. Sarah Millican is the new kid on the block for women in comedy. She tells it as it is and has great delivery and bang-on perfect timing.

Michelle Obama, she is so dignified and wears the most amazing Tahitian Pearls – I like that.

Kate Middleton, another dignified young lady who has manners and a good education, which is all you need in life – well, that and then marry a Prince.

Lulu Guinness, British designer who has an MBE. I love her – well, to be honest, I don't bloody know her but she designs the best handbags in the world.

Kylie has beaten cancer and bounced back time after time when her love life didn't work out. I guess she just never got over Michael Hutchence.

I like Kim Cattrall as Samantha Jones in Sex and the City – she's made being a slut rather classy.

Lady Gaga can't be overlooked. She's a modern day version of Madonna – a shrewd businesswoman who re-invents herself everytime.

Take a look around at the women who surround you: nurses, scientists, social workers, carers – the people who dedicate their lives to others. They are the true icons.

Sport has its female heroes. Dame Kelly Holmes has proved that our girls who compete these days can be very pretty as well as strong.

I used to think that Fatima Whitbread and Colonel Gadaffi were the same person. Come to think of it, I've never seen them both together. Not that I am advocating exercise. As Joan Rivers said: "If God had wanted women to bend he would have put diamonds in the gutter."

TOP 5 INSPIRATIONAL WOMEN - OVER 50

1. HELEN MIRREN
Prime Suspect star and voted
Body of the Year, at the age of 66, in 2011.

2. JUDI DENCH
How many BAFTAS can one woman get?

3. JOANNA LUMLEY
Multi-versatile actress, from comedy
to dramas.

4. SHIRLEY BASSEY
The girl from Tiger Bay looks younger
every year.

5. LULU
She gets better with age.
SHOUT about it, Lulu.

TEA FOR TWO

"Robert De Niro would be my
ideal companion.
He's such a dedicated actor and
he's gorgeous, too."

CHAPTER 3

Clubs and Campers

"Any comic who says he has never died on his arse is either lying or they never bloody work. The clubs were tough. The committees made sure that they were – no act had it easy."

IN 1980 I decided that it was time for me to make that break from The Tavern and leave the safety of the boys for the clubs.

I can honestly say that I have, in the main, had a great time. I've worked some right s*** holes but the people have been great. I did the rounds and I have had my share of good and bad.

My first husband Dave had a great idea about getting promo T-shirts for the bands that I regularly worked with embroidered with 'THERE'S ONLY ONE PAULINE DANIELS'.

On paper they looked really good. Dave had a steady supply and he wore his whenever we were working the clubs. He would sit proudly doing the sound for me with his polo shirt on show. One night we turned up at Lowton Labour Club in Leigh and as soon as I walked in through the door the Concert Fuhrer – sorry, I mean 'secretary' – said: "It's three spots: half eight, half nine and half ten."

I looked around and said: "Sorry, luv, I thought a dog had wandered in and you were talking to it."

"No, I'm talking to you", he snarled.

"Well," I said, "I DON'T do three spots. I'm a comedian and I only do ONE."

I then said to Dave: "Take the gear down." He was erecting the speakers at the time.

"Now, hang on a minute," Hitler said without subtitles. "There's no need to be hasty."

So, Dave carried on putting the speakers up.

"Perhaps you can do two spots."

"I only do one."

This guy is now annoying me big time.

"Get the gear down," I said.

Dave was like a yo-yo, up and down, down and up with the speakers – you get the picture – until this bolshy little dictator gave in and said: "Okay, one spot it is."

He then went on to introduce me and told the whole of the club that I had refused to do three spots and so the bingo was now thrown into chaos. Loud groans were heard all around the (full) house. I knew my fate was sealed. I was, as we say in showbiz circles, about to "die on my arse . . ."

And I did. Each gag landed on stoney ground. I watched as Dave gradually zipped up his jacket over his 'THERE'S ONLY ONE PAULINE DANIELS' T-shirt until it was zipped to his throat and the shirt was nowhere to be seen. I was buried.

Any comics who say they have never died on their arse are lying, or they never bloody work. The clubs were tough. The committees made sure that they were. No act had it easy.

Some concert secretaries would go out of their way to be b****** – and some others were fantastic.

I mainly encountered the good guys. I was working in a club called Moss Bank Labour in St Helens, and in those days we really had three spots to fit round the bingo. I had already done my first spot and been paid, and during my second section I caught my foot in between the lights and the edge of the stage – which was about eight foot high – and went arse-over-tit and fell off.

I was in a crumpled heap and the concert secretary asked: "Is there anyone out there who knows first aid?" As my ankle swelled before my eyes, the kind compere got two very strong fellas to pick me up and put me on a chair on the stage, and somebody from the bar brought an ice-soaked beer towel to put on my ankle while I finished my act. Well, come on, I had been paid.

I did a club in Newton-le-Willows and the racket from the audience was so bad I couldn't even hear the guy on keyboards playing 'Send in the Clowns' – ignorant b*******.

Peasley Cross Labour Club and Stubshaw Cross Labour Club (great Northern names) were jointly the worst places I ever did. Both of them were totally ruled by bingo and it didn't matter who you were, or what you did – you had to split your act to accommodate the bingo and the people were probably the rudest I have ever encountered.

Ah, well, apart from a horrible club I did in Scotland once. In the early 1980s, those little mining village venues were funny places. The women would come up to me after the show and ask how I got away with taking the mickey out of my husband without getting a good hiding. I found that really strange, but it was obvious that the women were living in a very chauvinistic state.

Anyway, this was an awful club. As you walked in, next to your name on the 'What's On' board was the amount of money you were getting, so I think that their mentality was "C'mon then, make us laugh."

I didn't.

They were also bingo mad. At the end of the night I

stole two balls out of the machine and it did give me some satisfaction to know that anyone who had 17 and 54 on their bloody bingo card would never win. I only hoped that it took them a while to discover the loss.

In 1981 I walked into a holiday camp for the first time since 1961, when Ringo Starr and I had become mates. This was a big deal for me. It was to be in the theatre at Pwllheli Butlin's and I had never ever worked in a theatre up to that point.

The nearest I had come to anything like that was Allinson's in Litherland and The Wooky Hollow, in Tuebrook – sadly, all gone now. Allinson's is now all new properties and The Wooky burnt down. Luckily, the grand piano and the sound system survived. That was lucky, wasn't it?

My first appearance at Allinson's was an exciting thing in our house. I was to go on the Sunday afternoon and do a noon show and then also perform the following Thursday, Friday and Saturday.

What we called 'complete weeks' in the cabaret clubs had well gone when I arrived in the business.

I had no idea that Sunday afternoon was when the lads all got in there to see what was coming up at the weekend, so they could bring the wife out, and also be treated to a stripper.

At the time I used to be a nice girl singer. I had a slinky long black gown, a skull cap all studded with diamantes and a lovely pink feather boa. I had also invited my mum and dad to see this spectacular event. ME, on at Allinson's.

What was I going to do about the stripper? The first

thing I did was ditch the boa. I looked out of the dressing room door and she had one and what she was doing with it had nothing to do with singing. I locked my mum and dad in my dressing room until she had finished. Isn't it funny how you start to protect your parents?

I wouldn't mind but they weren't that old. In fact, they would have been the same age as I am now, but still, I was only being nice. I didn't realise that strippers did Sunday lunch shows. I was soon to learn that I would work with a lot of strippers on a Sunday lunch.

So after this rude awakening, Butlin's was the Palladium to me. They had a stage manager, a little man who was very pompous, but I thought that this was quite some job and in those days it certainly was. The stage manager was the fella who did the Donkey Derby and served the hamburgers in the late-night bar. In 1981 this was a prestigious job.

I was working with 'The Nobodies', a comedy group a bit like the Black Abbotts. We had our call and I had a full band with a brass section and they could actually read music. In the clubs you were lucky if they could read the bloody Dandy, but these lads could quite honestly read fly s*** – it was wonderful.

We had two shows: one at 6pm and one at 8pm. There was a full supporting chorus of dancers. It was all teeth, tits and sequins. It was fantastic.

The dancers opened the show and then it was me. What a blast, musicians who could play and an audience who had come to watch a show and no sign of the man selling cockles to whom someone always shouted:

"Have you got any crabs on you, cock?"

And no bingo or raffle tickets being sold, no beer glasses or bottles making a racket, just me and the band. The audience was fantastic and I was a hit.

The Nobodies went on and everything was going fabulous till the sax player did a gag.

"A little lad went for an ice cream and the woman said, 'Do you want crushed nuts?' and he said, 'Do you want your tits blowing off?'"

Now the audience loved it, but the stage manager was angry. He was pacing up and down backstage, saying: "In all the years I have been in the theatre nobody, but nobody, has ever said TITS on my stage."

Well, they were The Nobodies. The lads were very apologetic and promised it wouldn't happen in the next show. The offending member of the group said it wasn't his fault . . . he was sober.

That started my many years of work with Butlin's and I had the most amazing time between 1981 and 1992, which was when I called it a day.

SONGS TO AVOID WHEN YOU'VE BEEN DUMPED

1. Winner Takes it All – Abba

2. It Should Have Been Me – Yvonne Fair

3. Tell Me on A Sunday – Marti Webb

4. All By Myself – Eric Carmen

5. D.I.V.O.R.C.E. – Tammy Wynette
or Billy Connolly

6. I Heard It Through the Grapevine
– Marvin Gaye

7. End of the World – Skeeta Davis

8. I Will Always Love You
– Whitney Houston

9. Any bloody country and western song

10. If You're Looking For A Way Out
– Odyssey

 **SONGS TO LISTEN TO HAVING BEEN DUMPED**

1. Shaddup yer Face – Joe Dolce

2. I Will Survive – Gloria Gaynor

3. Don't Stop Me Now – Queen

4. The Only Way is Up – Yazz

5. Man I Feel Like a Woman
– Shania Twain

6. These Boots are Made for Walking
– Nancy Sinatra

7. Moving On Up – M People

8. Girls Just Wanna Have Fun
– Cyndi Lauper

9. Feelin' Good – Nina Simone

10. Grain of Salt – Toby Keith

who's that Woman?

"The business was and still
is dominated by men,
but then I have always been
one of the boys and I enjoyed
it that way."

I WORE out many a car doing my summer seasons, travelling more than 2,000 miles a week, a lot of the time on my own.

I recall coming home one Friday afternoon. I walked into the kitchen, where Sarah and her dad were sat at the kitchen table. They didn't say a word.

I opened the washing machine, put my clothes in and Sarah said: "Hey dad, who's that woman putting her stuff in our machine?" I was maybe neglecting my family a little. It's hard though when you are the bread winner and the mother. You tend to make up for moments that you should have, by buying 'things', but you can't ever make up the time, unfortunately.

I then decided that Sarah would go with me for the whole of her six weeks school holiday – that'll teach you! In the main she enjoyed being with me, but she hated those awful chalets. Why they had to artex the walls I have no idea. But every time you turned over in bed you took three layers of skin off your arms.

When you know the way things are, you get wise and you take your own pillows and toilet paper.

They still have that awful shiny Izal bog roll now, you know. I mean, you can maybe put up with it for a week, but when you are doing 26 weeks your arse could end up like a blood orange.

I made lots of friends in the 11 years I did Butlin's and I even defected for a few years and did Pontins. It was not the same. It never was: it thought it was a cut above, but it just lacked that extra bit of magic that Butlin's had. I worked with some stars at Butlin's, the biggest being Bob Monkhouse. I did my first telly show, but then didn't see Bob for a while. He used to do the midnight cabaret and I did the earlier show and then got on the road home. I arrived at Minehead one night and there was a note from Bob saying he had seen me on the telly and thought I was great. Now he didn't have to do that but he did – that was nice.

I worked with some fabulous musicians there. One year in particular – 1984 – the lads were nearly all from South Wales. Terry on drums – he was 19 at the time and absolutely brilliant. Harry on trumpet, Beefy on saxophone, Ritchie on guitar and poor Dave the keyboard player, who had to keep that unruly lot in order. This was at Pwllheli and it was also the year I did my Thursday nights with Paul Duval – a well-respected cabaret performer – in the Spanish Bar.

I remember us arriving that first week for a band call, and we were both knocked out with the lads – they were superb. we knew this was going to be a great season, and it was.

The week for me consisted of: Saturday, Scarborough; Sunday, Skegness; Monday, Bognor: Tuesday, Minehead; Wednesday, Barry Island; Thursday, Pwllheli; Friday, Pontins Prestatyn, otherwise known as 'the toss pot'.

Paul Duval and I used to travel together along with Dave my husband and, no, there was never anything between us. I had to listen to Paul's moaning. That's all he seemed to do. In fact, Dave used to say if it wasn't for Duval there would never have been a depression. We always had to stop at Bala so he could be sick, every week the same place and time.

He was eventually moved to the front seat and that

helped. I sat in the back then and could nod off and not have to listen to his moaning. I don't mean awful moaning. It was just the usual about bills and not seeming to have the money to cover them.

I always thought he was happily married, but then he thought Dave and I were, too. The truth is, cracks were starting to appear in my marriage although it did drag on for another seven years after that.

It's funny though, if you're away from home for a great amount of time you can put up with the crap for a few months of the year, which is exactly what I did.

One thing I used to do for all the bands at Butlin's was the 'Cider Run'. I travelled from Minehead to Barry every Wednesday and the lads in all the bands used to put their Scrumpy order in. My car smelt like a hooch wagon and I felt like Granny Clampett transporting all this booze from one camp to the next.

I would deliver the cider when I arrived, and the lads would make it last for as long as they could. Not so with the Pwllheli boys, though. One night I gave these lads their ale and then went on stage, opened with a song and then sent the lads off while I did the comedy.

When they came back things were strange. I introduced the song, 'I Don't Know How To Love Him' from Jesus Christ Superstar. The grand introduction began . . . and then the strangest noise in the world, as if someone had sat on a trumpet, or even ate one – and then farted. I turned and looked at Harry the trumpeter and then at Beefy and the lights were on, but nobody was at home. They were totally rat-arsed. Marvellous.

Now Harry couldn't half drink. I remember him being

drunk one afternoon in the pit in the theatre and he sat next to Terry, who was the loudest drummer in the world – but even he couldn't wake him. These lads were out of it. Needless to say, after that occasion, they wouldn't be given their Scrumpy until I had been on and finished my performance.

I remember so well that Paul Duval (Kenny, who went on to become Husband Number Three), used to do 'Amor', the Julio Iglesias song. Before Paul sang it he used to tell the audience that Julio had underwear thrown at him on stage. So backstage, I used to get all sorts of stuff out of my clothes bag and chuck it at him. I started to sew extra cups into an old bra and throw that at him. One week he was singing "Amor, Amor", as the bra landed at his feet, He picked it up and sang "there's four!" with perfect timing. What a team we were, even then.

On the last week I threw all sorts at him and one of the items was a thong, which I would like to point out I never wore. I tried it and realised it was like dental floss for your arse. I couldn't think of anything more uncomfortable than having a bit of string stuck up your bum all day. You'd be forever trying to yank it out – not very attractive. I chucked this thong and Paul threw it back – only, it landed on Beefy's saxophone and he refused to give it back. About six years ago I met a guy who knew Beefy and he told me he still has that thong wrapped around his sax.

You will have gathered by now that I spent most of my time with men. The business was and still is dominated by men, but then I have always been one of the boys and I enjoyed it that way. I love to entertain the girls but I have never been one for 'girls' nights out'. I have always enjoyed a pint and a conversation about football, and even been lucky to perform for some of my favourite footballers over the years at their testimonials. I have met some really nice ones. I met a few a***holes too, but then we all meet those in every walk of life.

One of my favourites is the lovely Dave Hickson. His wife Pat used to be a model for Norman Hartnell, so I suppose they were the 'Posh and Becks' of their day. Now, for those of you who know nothing at all about footie, Dave played for all three Mersey clubs: Liverpool, Everton and Tranmere Rovers.

His heart though is with Everton, so much so that a few seasons ago he collapsed at a match. Just before the kick-off. Actor Neil Caple – Marty in Brookside, and a good mate of mine – sent me a text to let me know what had happened as he sits next to Dave at the match.

They rushed Dave to hospital and the nurses swear that the only thing that pulled him through was the fact that Everton won. Well, not only won, but beat their opposition by seven goals to one, and the nurses kept coming and telling him: "They've scored again, Dave!"

Back in the days of those summer seasons, I spent most of my time with the lads but I was always with my husband as well, so temptation never got in the way. Well, almost never.

I was always a bit of a shop steward and I'll speak up for anyone. I won't have any friends of mine or family hurt for the world – I've always been the same really.

I was very upset when I arrived for a show at Butlin's one night, to discover that Robbie the entertainment manager had banned the lads in the band from drinking in the late-night bar. He was convinced that Harry had his eye on his girlfriend – which turned out to be complete tosh because she ran off with another woman.

In my infinite wisdom, I rang the big boss and asked him if the lads were okay to go for a drink with me. He said that would be fine, so we were all there having a late-night bevvy when Robbie the little Hitler walked in and shouted at them all. I told him that I had got permission and he left with his tail between his legs. Sadly, he took it out on the lads for the rest of the season.

Thanks to Butlin's I was successful and in 1990 I had another fabulous summer season, and I met my best mate Colin Cattle. He was the band leader that year and a bass player, unusual for a musical director, but he was s*** hot. The rest of the band were great, too, but Colin and I just hit it off immediately. Ricky McCabe and Tony Birmingham, who were managing the show at the time, were trying to find a speciality act to complete the line-up so we could take it on the road.

They were leaving no stone unturned. I went with them to see a woman with a massive snake, which she would wrap around herself as she stripped. It has to be said, she was the size of a small island. I'm sure she was a lovely woman but, honestly, people would pay for her to get dressed. We couldn't really take anymore so we left when she was down to her underwear. The poor snake looked like it was going to be smothered in rolls of flesh. I wonder how many snakes she went through in her career.

One cold and wet Wednesday afternoon, Ricky, Tony and I met at the BAT club in Bootle to audition an act called 'The Helmet Brothers'. The lads arrived and gave their music tape to the DJ, and then went into the dressing room.

Five minutes later the music started – Mike Oldfield's 'In Dulce Jubilo' – and on the stage came these two naked men wearing only German helmets, socks, arm bands and a Hitler moustache. Tony choked on his tea and Ricky and I were just bent in two laughing at these guys covering their 'bits' with balloons. As the routine hotted up they burst the balloons and then blew up new ones that were strategically placed in their armbands. It was the funniest thing I had ever seen.

Gary Helmet was a bit rotund, mainly bald, but what hair was left was ginger. Dave, his brother, was skinny with glasses. These boys were not the Chippendales. Tony was mortified: "We can't use them, we'll get raided", was all he could say. Ricky and I couldn't speak, they were hysterical. We had to have them.

The Pauline Daniels Really Rude Show was now complete. We toured for the best part of six months and had a ball. The clubs were always busy in those days and I have been all over the country to see just who has got the best sense of humour.

Strangely enough, Liverpool has an equal sense of humour to Glasgow, Newcastle and Cardiff, all very busy ports in their day, so I have come to the conclusion that it's the sea air that makes everyone a comedian in Liverpool. It's the only place in the world where the audience are 90 per cent likely to be funnier than you. You have got to get in quick if you think you are going to get a heckler. In the 1980s hecklers were brilliant. They were never nasty, they just used to like to be the centre of attention and if you had a good one, you could get half of your act out of them.

In the 1990s it all changed. Hecklers became quite aggressive, and the only clever thing they could ever come up with was "F*** off."

You can't really give a clever answer back to that and, of course, being a woman meant they all thought they were quite big shouting that at you. Fortunately for me, by the time the Nineties had come round, I had learnt quite an extensive foul language vocabulary myself, so they still didn't win.

When I die, if I have to have a memorial stone, I would want part of a review that was written about me in a play called 'Dirty Dustin' by a well-respected theatre critic who hated the show with a passion. At the end of the write-up he wrote: '5/10 . . . Smut Fest.'

I want that on the front and then PTO (wish I could turn over, but I'd be dead) and on the back the two 10 out of 10 reviews I was given for playing Shirley Valentine.

Dead good.

TOP 5 IDEAL OLYMPIC EVENTS

1. Slow jump.

2. Short jump.

3. Low jump.

4. Race to the hospitality bar.

5. Having a shower with the lads.

D'YA THINK I'M SEXY?

No ... Not at all. I was never a Tomboy. I loved pretty dresses. I was a lovely little girl – never wanted to get my hands dirty in the gutter.
It is interesting. I heard once that someone thought I was sexy on stage – all that that domineering thing. I am bossy by nature – maybe some people like that. I have played some sexy women such as Mae West. But me? No, I am playing a role.
At the end of the day though, who knows what sexy is? Beauty is in the eye – and ears – of the beholder. Are you sexy, dear reader?

TV and Traumas

"I've been to so many auditions, I'm beginning to think my name is NEXT."

BEFORE actually doing any telly as an act, I did a couple of 'extra' jobs.

I'm not a Ricky Gervais fan but that programme Extras is so accurate and true to life. I soon discovered that the extras were made up of old club acts who actually believed that because they were doing this work that they were bona fide performers. I'm sorry, but most of them were failed acts that no one had ever heard of.

My first job was quite exciting. It was the BBC classic Boys from the Black Stuff, in 1982. It was the second episode and I was to be at a funeral. Dead loss, I hear you say.

I am the first person out of the door on the way to the service, I look up the street and then put my umbrella up . . . worthy of a BAFTA.

My second job was the last episode and yet again it was a bloody funeral – I must have one of those gobs. The director, Philip Saville, asked us all to cross ourselves as the funeral cars passed the houses. I asked which way I was to cross myself as I am not a Catholic.

He said it didn't matter but, you see, even then I was a perfectionist. I couldn't do it unless it was right.

I met Mr Saville years later at an audition for something else (I've been to so many auditions I'm beginning to think my name is 'NEXT').

He remembered me as the one who argued with him – I never got that job!

My next two 'extra' roles finished me off for good and I swore I would never do it again.

I did a television drama called Artemis and it was about people left after a nuclear fallout. We filmed it at the Albert Dock before they all became trendy flats and shops and the Tate Gallery.

It was dreary down there then. I was never the kind of kid who played in the gutter, because I hated getting dirt on me in any shape or form. This job was horrendous. Everybody had stick-on sores and boils and the funniest thing happened at the end of the shoot.

We were all walking back into the hotel to get changed and the make-up girl said to one fella: "Don't forget to let us have that nose back." It was his real nose, bless him.

That was an awful job, but the last one I did was to take the biscuit. It was for BBC Wales and we were to be picked up at 4am in Liverpool and driven to Caernarvon Castle to re-enact the Investiture of Prince Charles.

It was set in the Sixties so we all had micro miniskirts on, and it was at the height of a beautiful summer. All the dresses were flimsy and thin and, as I say, very short. This, however, was being done in November.

Get the picture? It was bleedin' freezin'. By the end of the day I had the worst dose of flu I think I have ever had in my life. That made my mind up. I would never EVER be an extra again.

I would never have to stand around all day while the main actors had lovely little trailers with heaters to stay in. I would never wait at the back of a queue while the main actors got the best of the catering wagon while I didn't.

Now, whenever I do any telly work, I never expect anybody to wait till I've got MY food. I let everyone in.

I don't let them 'get a warm' in my trailer. Well, there's never enough room . . . honest, to God.

In a funny way I was a bit lucky. You normally have to be in this business for years before you get a shot at doing a bit of telly, but it was 1983 when it knocked on my trailer door.

I had done an audition before for Central TV, but only as a female vocalist. I had moved on since then. I was still singing but I was telling gags in between my songs. I have no idea how it happened because it was a few years ago. I couldn't say a word between songs before, but now I was "funny" and really pissing off the male comics.

I was working with lots of them and I'm not saying that they weren't funny – they were – but, all of a sudden, this woman had arrived. I was novel and I was BLOODY GOOD.

I was also discovering that women were not really supposed to be funny and guess what – it wasn't just the male comics who were getting pissed off, it was the male population in general.

It seems that although I was using hubby Dave as a stooge, whatever I said about him seemed to be the truth about every man on the planet.

The women, on the other hand, loved it. They had spent all of their club-going life listening to men being totally chauvinistic, ripping their wives and mother-in-laws to bits and now, what the hell had happened?

Here's a woman shooting from the lip, telling it how it is, and if a man moves while she's up there doing it, she will verbally massacre him.

CHAPTER 5 – TV AND TRAUMAS

This is where my reputation started. The sad thing was I was stopping men moving everywhere – not just to the toilet, which has probably caused many a man to have prostrate trouble later in life – but also to the bar. Now, this isn't good. When beer sales drop something has to go.

Fortunately, I realised before it was too late – a concert secretary at Kirkby RAOB club told me. In fact, it was the reason they wouldn't book me any more. So I learned to control it and make sure the tables were full of ale before I started picking on men.

I also found a great heckler-stopper when I had a bunch of young men who I thought were going to get a bit out of control. I would make a bee line for them after studying the table, seeing which was the one with the loudest mouth and I would just nick his pint and down it in one. GULP . . . GLUG. Wipe the foam from my mouth. A sure fire way of shutting them up.

First of all they weren't going to mess about with a woman who could down a pint like that and they weren't going to risk having their beer stolen – so it always worked.

I went through a stage of not wearing glasses on stage and couldn't wear contact lenses. One night I picked up a pint of Guinness – not pure genius, a big mistake. I had to go through with it and as it was going down I could feel it coming back up again.

If I'd have had a packet of peanuts that night I swear I could have farted and pebble dashed three houses on the way home.

I still meet men today who are actually quite proud of

the fact that I have, at some time or other, drank their beer. I suppose I also gained a bit of respect from the boys for downing a pint. It did, however, help to pile on loads of weight which I struggled to lose at a later date, but at the time it was important.

Of course, having a bit of weight, not being a swan and taking the piss out of men, always makes you a big hit with the girls.

I have – over the years – gained a lot of women fans. I am so grateful to them all. Even when I lost a load of weight, some of the women would say to me that they were on diets because I was an inspiration. Once you are a sister you are a sister for life. Thanks girls. I love you all.

The lads, however, are not so kind. I was working at The Adelphi Hotel in Liverpool in 1986 and I was in the main ballroom, which is a very big room, and I was at the stage end wandering with a radio microphone. I was wearing a black lace skirt suit and I noticed a man staggering towards me.

He obviously didn't notice the microphone and thought I was a member of staff. He was drunk, to say the least, and when he got up to me he said: "Hey girl, where's the gents?"

I replied: "I think they are at the back, love".

He clocked the microphone, studied my face and said: "Aren't you that comedienne, what's her name, er, Pauline Daniels?"

I said "Yes, that's right".

He said: "I saw you on TV AM, f****** hell, girl, you look rough first thing in the morning."

Follow that!

I was now really making a name for myself in the clubs and I also had an audition for Central TV.

On the night before the telly test I sat with David and we went through my act to find a really strong 10 -minute section and a couple of good songs to top and tail the sessions with.

We had been recording the act over a few weeks and had now edited a section that was perfect and I was going to listen to it all day before the audition. I also took it upon myself to clean all my jewellery, sparkling and ready for the big gig. We left everything on the floor in the lounge and went to bed.

When we got up everything was gone, including the whole of the kitchen window. During the night someone had broken in and stolen all my jewellery, the video recorder, portable telly – and the edited tape that I was going to use for the audition.

What a s*** day. It got worse.

We had a lovely Labrador who hadn't made a sound while we were being robbed. She couldn't, because the b****** had poisoned her and later that day she died.

I didn't give in though. They weren't going to beat me. I thought: "Well, things can't get any worse than this?" and I said: "Look on the bright side, Pauline."

It was bad. I was talking to myself.

We were asleep when this all happened. We could have been hurt in our beds. We could have been killed. I thought: "Get out there and get a TV programme out of it . . ."

And I did. The show must go on.

Strangely enough, I had auditioned for one of these Central TV people before as a singer, and he had told my agent: "She's good, but she's no dolly bird, is she?"

Now, the same man, along with a very, wet-behind-the-ears Nigel Lythgoe, decided that as a funny bird it didn't matter what I looked like – and so they gave me a shot. The show was called Saturday Royal and it came from the fabulous Nottingham Royal Theatre.

I did two episodes and it was the show that also gave Gary Wilmot and Duncan Norvelle their start. I worked with Duncan years later on the Ricky Tomlinson Laughter Tour.

The Saturday Royal gang rehearsed in the old Pinewood Studios and I had the legendary Sid and Dick (Green and Hill) – who had made their name years previously writing for Morecambe and Wise – now writing for me.

The man who had accused me of not being a dolly bird asked would I sing a song in the musical finale. I said to him: "Bill, I'm not a dolly bird." It was wonderful watching him go the colour of a smacked arse.

That musical finale helped me to do a lot more, so, in a funny way, I thank him. Lionel Blair hosted the show and we really did gel together, so much so that even I called him LiLi.

I did commit the unforgiveable crime, though. I was in the canteen and Lionel introduced me to Danny La Rue. They sat down with their lunches and I said: "I saw your show in Margate with Ronnie Corbett."

He smiled: "Oh really. Did you like it"?

"Yes", said I. "It was great. I was about 11 at the time." SILENCE.

In the last show of the Saturday Royal series, I was mortified that in the finale all the girls were wearing top hat and tails with fishnet tights.

I looked terrible, my arse looked like a waffle. All the other girls on the show, who were mainly dancers, had legs that went up to their armpits. I'm still five foot tall with little fat legs (always will be).

Well, they are good pins, but not put up against all of those long-legged cows. What's another word for bitch? In the dictionary it says: "See Pauline Daniels."

I fought with producer, director and wardrobe mistress but they all insisted that I wore the same outfit. Would it have hurt for me to have had a skirt?

I had been a success on this programme. I'd sung, been funny, dueted with LiLi and now they wanted to wreck it all by making me look a total blert. I spoke to my agent and family and they all knew how upset I was, so they knew not to say anything in the bar. Afterwards, when it was all over, I thought GREAT! It will never be mentioned again.

Six months later and I am in a club with a male singer, whom I'd worked with lots of times and liked very much. We were stood at the bar and he said: "Look at that," as he pointed to the large net hanging from the ceiling that most clubs used to have for the balloons at New Year. "That looks like your arse in them fishnet tights." That was in 1983. I married that man in 2002 – I haven't forgiven him though.

My next big break in television was appearing on Wogan. Sir Terry Wogan – a national treasure and all that, to be sure. A couple of nights after Princess Anne had been on, I was with Rick Springfield, Duran Duran, Patrick Duffy and the American Comedy governor, Bob Hope. This was a really BIG coup.

I was the only person I hadn't heard of.

I had done The Comedians and we knew it was definitely going out on air. Johnny Hamp had recorded a few women, Marti Caine, Sue Pollard and Victoria Wood – but they had never made it to the telly, the reason being that none of them actually told gags. Although Granada was desperate to have a woman on, she really needed to 'patter like a man' – which is, thankfully, exactly what I did.

So we had something to plug in 1985 on the Wogan show. It used to be on three nights a week and anybody who was anybody would appear on this programme. I will never forget Terry's introduction that evening: "Tonight is the night, the stars fell on Shepherd's Bush. We have – direct from Canada – rock sensation, Rick Springfield . . ."

Studio audience: "Hoorah!"

"We have Bobby Ewing himself all the way from windy Southfork, Dallas . . ."

"HOORAH!"

"Duran Duran will be here to perform, for the first time, their James Bond theme soundtrack View to a Kill . . ."

"SCREAM! HOORAH! SCREAM!"

"We have the King of Comedy, Bob Hope . . ."

"EVEN BIGGER HOORAH!"

"And we have some home-grown talent, in the form of Pauline Daniels . . ."

"WHOOOOOOO? Who the bloody hell is that?"

It was a great experience being on the chat show but I was also so pleased to have been in the hospitality room with those massive names: Ricky McCabe was with me and Dave, and we were all in awe of everyone.

Terry introduced me to Patrick Duffy. I just looked him in the belly button (he's massive) and said:

"Hiya, I watch yer on a Wednesday." What an idiot.

He was absolutely gorgeous. I have to say he looked so handsome and didn't have make-up to go on stage, so if you can imagine how harsh the TV lights are, yet he looked perfect without any help. I, however, had been in make up since three o'clock that afternoon.

I was a bit pissed off with Simon Le Bon of Duran Duran. My daughter, Sarah, was a big fan in those days and I asked him for an autograph and he said he was too busy. Well, that was the start of their demise, and Sarah never ever bought another Duran Duran album. I was so ignorant, though – I thought Rick Springfield was Dusty's brother.

I was then introduced to Bob Hope and I spoke to him for what seemed like 20 minutes. It was probably only five, but all I remember him saying was that it was tough for a woman in comedy – and that one of his best friends in the business was Phyllis Diller. I was so in awe that my gob had dropped into my shoes by this time.

When I went back to my agent Ricky McCabe, he asked me what Bob Hope had said and I couldn't remember a thing. I felt so good that night because, after the show, I had to be flown to Newcastle to do yet another TV programme, a regional one this time with Nina Myskow.

She wanted me to tell a joke in front of Mary Whitehouse, Media Clean Up Britain Campaigner, to prove that it wasn't always the joke that was dirty, but very often your own mind.

Well, we proved it. I started the gag, Mrs Whitehouse's face was like thunder and then, by the time the punchline came, she laughed. I had already recorded The Comedians by the time I did Wogan but that was probably the scariest telly ever.

At this stage of my career I was hated by all the local comedians. Not only was I getting more work than them but, of course, I was standing out like a sore thumb because I was a woman. Despite this, I still wasn't commanding the same money as they were, I know that much.

I turned up at Granada studios and was definitely not constipated, if you know what I mean. I spent a little time in make up and then quite a while pulling the knives out of my back. It was quite obvious that I wasn't really welcome.

There were, however, two comics who did help: Vince Earl, probably better known as Ron Dixon in Brookside, who was a mate of mine. We worked for the same agent at the time and he was going to record The Comedians a week before me, so he very kindly took me with him so I could see exactly what went on, and prepare me for my own recording the week after.

The other helpful comic was Stan Boardman. Stan was hosting the show which, if anyone can remember, was quite a stark set with a microphone and a live audience. Everyone had cue cards and Stan gave me a big tip: "Don't write your cue cards in a way that anyone else can read them."

Years before, Bernard Manning used to host the shows and they would record three a week – that was 30 comedians – and then edit it all together. All the cue cards were lined up underneath the camera man, and, of course, there wasn't a joke Manning didn't know.

When he spotted a gag he liked on another comic's cue card he would do it. Nine out of 10 times when he did that HIS would be the gag that was aired and the other comic would go to pieces. So all my cue cards were in code.

I've got to be honest and say that apart from Vince Earl and Stan Boardman helping me out on that show, those bloody knives hurt. I was stabbed in the front.

In 1991, Granada decided to do another series of The Comedians. They didn't want to put the 'old' style comics on this time, they wanted to show how far comedy had come. We had already been bombarded by the likes of Ben Elton (always gave me a bloody headache that man) so Granada wanted people who were still doing the clubs, but had not been on any of the old series.

They searched for a woman – and searched, and searched, and eventually they rang me and asked me to do it. I broke the mould because not only was I the only woman, again, but I was also the only comic to do BOTH series.

We were all told to dress down for the show – no

sequins this time – to prove that Granada was bang up to date. I chose to wear a woman's dinner suit and they were happy. I did my sound check and wardrobe check and everyone was happy. Then, as I was introduced I had put on the biggest pair of diamanté earrings that went right up my ears and there was nothing they could do about it. I'd always been known for 'glitz and glamour' and I wasn't going to change now.

All I had to do was make sure I was that good so they couldn't edit me out. I was, and they didn't. Unfortunately it only ran for one series. Stand-up comedy was changing and variety was about to disappear.

TOP 5 DREADED LIFT COMPANIONS

1. NICK CLEGG.
He's a puppet. Although, having said that, he'd be very quiet because he wouldn't have David Cameron's hand up his arse.

2. JORDAN/KATIE PRICE.
She deserves real credit for bringing up a child with a disability, but she is a self-opinionated bad role model for any young woman. If I spoke to her she might give as good as she gets, but I've been at it a lot longer than her. Trust me, I would win.

3. CILLA BLACK
Her whiney voice would get on my nerves. If she did a Cliff Richard and started to sing I'd probably throttle her.

4. TIM HENMAN
Our former Wimbledon tennis hope is so boring he shouldn't even be here.

5. ANNE WIDDECOMBE
There'd be no room.

Funny girl Pauline gets in on the act

By Gerard Dempsey

A LAUGH-A-MINUTE housewife is poised to topple television's last bastion of male supremacy.

After 17 years of The Comedians enter The Comedienne. . . .

Pauline Daniels, cabaret-singer-turned-comic, bursts on to the small screen as a wise-cracking newcomer on the same bill as veterans Frank Carson, George Roper, Bernard Manning and Stan Boardman.

She makes her Granada debut in the first of a new seven-part series of the award-winning show on June 1.

And the programme boss who has steadfastly steered clear of professional funny women since the show's launch in 1971 says he couldn't be more delighted. . . .

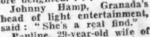

Johnny Hamp, Granada's head of light entertainment, said : "She's a real find."

Pauline, 29-year-old wife of a self-employed electrician, was a professional singer before she turned to comedy four years ago.

She said at her home at Ellesmere Port, Wirral, that her voice packed in during a club concert in Blackpool, " so because I couldn't sing I could still talk, I just told jokes."

Booked

The audience loved her, and she is already booked for two dates with The Comedians.

She has created a new tele-character, the indomitable Anastasia, mother-of-16 from downtown Toxteth, five times married, bingo barmy, with a beehive hairdo instead of a brain.

Says Pauline : " I have Anastasia boasting : 'After 15 years on the dole, they've finally given Fred a job.'

" And her mate sympathises : ' Just when you wa getting on your feet '

laugh a minute

THE ARTS

Women steal the show

Phil Cutts

THEATRE

Comedians
Everyman, Liverpool

As a lesson in the tenacity of sexist prejudice this female version of Trevor Griffiths's play would be hard to beat. Girl comedians may have been proliferating in the 12 years since the first production of *Comedians*. But the piece itself seems so exclusively masculine — both in its comic material, and in its portrait of a class of van drivers, labourers and milkmen hoping for a showbusiness break — as to defeat any idea of a switch in gender.

If the author had any qualms about this, he swallowed them when Kate Rowland sent him a video of the "school for comediennes" which she ran at Liverpool last year; and, in collaboration with the company, he reworked the text for the production Miss Rowland has now directed at the Everyman.

The first surprise, in an evening of suprises, is that the first act remains almost unchanged. The off-stage jobs of the class have largely been edited out; and at the announced arrival of the London talent scout, he changes from "an agent's man" to "an agent (sinister pause) and a man". Otherwise the improvizations and tongue-twisters, and the comic friction between the competitors, sound as if they have been written for these abrasive Liverpool ladies.

If anything, they strengthen the reality of the scene. Originally, Griffiths undermined his argument against comic stereotyping by introducing a stage full of stereotypes. But when the Irishmen and the Jew change sex, they simply turn into people.

There remains the question of their teacher, a veteran stand-up comic who, throughout the play, never cracks a joke. As originally played by Jimmy Jewel this did not matter: you knew he could if he wanted to. Ann

Mitchell does not have that advantage: but as Ella Waters, the Lancashire Lass, she radiates a fervour that is all the more potent for its subdued, unsmiling contrast with high-charged egos exploding all round her.

The second act, credited jointly to Griffiths and to five members of the company, shows the girls doing their stuff for a club audience during a break from bingo. With the exception of the revolutionary finale the routines have been almost wholly rewritten. But, while substituting jokes about Irish husbands and other objects of female scorn for the original targets, they present the same inner drama of resistance or capitulation to the commercial talent scout.

Carving her way through a choice set of taboo topics: Pauline Daniels in the all-female *Comedians*

An added fascination is the presence in the company of two professional comedians: Jenny Lecoat, who brilliantly takes on the role of the only comically untalented member of the group; and Pauline Daniels, who lives up to her local reputation as Queen of Liverpool's club-circuit by carving her way through a choice set of taboo topics: she is rude, aggressive, and side-splittingly funny.

Finally, Cheryl Maiker steps into the long shadow of Jonathan Pryce (the original star pupil) with her nightmare Grock routine. Miss Maiker has nothing like Pryce's dangerous magnetism and does not dominate the rest of the play as he did. But in this scene, she out-classes him. A white-faced clown punk, she is

neither man nor woman: only a spectre of hate-filled destitution, who approaches her two elegantly dressed doll victims with snarling pleasantries, shakes them into laughter, and leaves the man with blood seeping down his gleaming white shirt front. I do not know how this production would work elsewhere. In Liverpool it makes your hair stand on end.

The point of this is blurred in the last act, which is played in a portentous, dragging undertone, and shows Miss Maiker — the author's intended victor — losing hands down to the stronger personality of Miss Mitchell. Otherwise, the show does not put a foot wrong.

Irving Wardle

Bursting onto the small screen as a wise-cracking newcomer on 'The Comedians' – a review from the Daily Express in 1985. Above, The Times described me as "rude, aggressive and side-splittingly funny", in a production of 'Comedians' at The Everyman, Liverpool, 1987

91

CHAPTER 6

Treading the Red Boards

"I cried because, as a child, I wanted to do this. I cried because I had actually done it, despite not having any formal training, and I wept because I was all alone . . ."

AFTER I had done 'Saturday Royal', I received a very interesting phone call saying Tommy Steele had been on, asking whether I would be interested in going for an audition to The London Palladium.

Wow! I had grown up with 'Sunday Night at the London Palladium' and now I was going for an audition for the woman at the beginning of 'Singing in the Rain', the Hedda Hopper-type character.

I arrived and there were about 30 other women there. I didn't have a clue what to do and felt I was completely out of my depth. I listened to the others go in and sing a song, but they all seemed pretty ordinary to me. When it was my turn I just hit them with 'If They Could See Me Now' from 'Sweet Charity'. They seemed impressed and when I went backstage, one actress said: "We might as well all bugger off home, what a voice." I was flattered, but still didn't have a clue what I was doing.

A very camp guy with a clipboard came backstage and read out 15 names, one of which was mine, and then he said thank you to the others. It was dance time – Jesus Christ!

I'd never danced, well, only on a table half pissed. We were all led back on stage and a choreographer took us through a routine. They all had jazz shoes and leg warmers on while I had the shoes I'd come in. Still, I'd got this far, so what the hell?

I watched and followed and, if there was a step I wasn't sure of, I made it up. We were all sent back again and out came the guy with the clipboard and read out four names. Mine was still there. This time we were reading and this I could do. At the end of the afternoon we were all told that they would let us know.

When I got back Ricky told me that there was me and another woman called Pip Hinton up for the job. I knew that name. She had been in 'Crackerjack' when I was a kid. Bloody hell, I'd hit the big time!

I waited weeks and weeks until finally they came back saying that they had gone with Pip Hinton as she had the more experience of the two of us. I wasn't too disappointed. After all, I had loads of work, I didn't need the job, I just wanted it, and hey, what the hell, I lost out to a woman who knew what she was doing and had been in 'Crackerjack'.

I'd loved the Palladium though and all of a sudden I had the bug. I really did now want to do theatre and all those years as a little girl, telling my mum that I wanted to be an actress, I had been a midge's dick away from that dream.

About eight months later I did a variety show at the Palladium. The manager was lovely, and he came to my dressing room and told me that Tommy Steele had said that the reason I didn't get the job was that there were only two stars and I might just have shone a little too much.

Now he didn't have to say that, did he? I stood on the stage where Judy Garland had fell over years before when she was drunk and unable to perform.

I wandered all over that theatre thinking, taking it all in and really wanting to be in a musical of some sort. I had no idea that it wouldn't be too long before I was in a musical, and it wouldn't be too long before I was working with the actress whose dressing room

I was borrowing that Sunday Variety night. Her name was Danielle Carson, and she was playing the Debbie Reynolds role in 'Singing in the Rain', which was still running.

But that was it for me. I had tasted a very small piece of the real theatre and I wanted much, much more. However, I was earning a really good living doing the summer seasons and working the clubs and the difference in pay was colossal. I could earn in one night for an hour's stand-up what I could earn for a whole week – six days and eight shows, matinees on Wednesdays and Saturdays – in the theatre. I still wanted it though!

My first big break on the theatre stage came from The Liverpool Playhouse. I got a call from Ian Kellgren, who was the artistic director at the time, and he simply said: "How would you fancy being in a musical?"

Now, bear in mind that I didn't know this man and he had only seen me do some telly – we were both a bit blind. I asked what the part was and when he said Mama Morton in 'Chicago' I couldn't believe it.

There was only one problem. I had booked a holiday in Greece with the family: Dave, Sarah, mum, dad and nan. Nan had never in her life been abroad and she was 80. Mind you, on her 80th birthday she went on a day trip to Blackpool with some pensioners and came back with her ears pierced. What next? She was likely to come back from Greece with a bloody tattoo. It must run in the family.

I now had a big dilemma on my hands: yes, I wanted to go to Greece, but I wanted Chicago more.

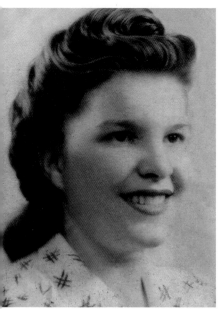

Dear Doreen: My beautiful Mum in 1946

Very Handsome Dad: The black sheep of the Malam family, 'Copper' left for the Army in 1939. He was truly golden to me

My Nan Doris: She made everything special. Not a single day goes by when I don't think about her

Family Gathering: Mum, Dad and me at Butlin's, 1966

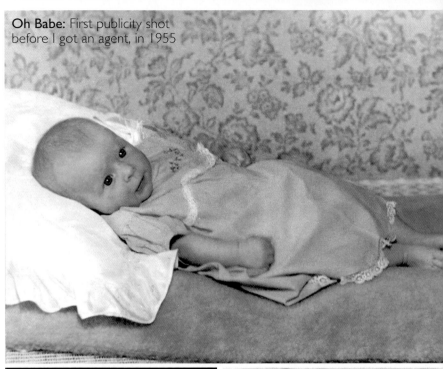

Oh Babe: First publicity shot before I got an agent, in 1955

Clause In My First Contract: I'm the one without the beard at Blacklers Grotto, 1959

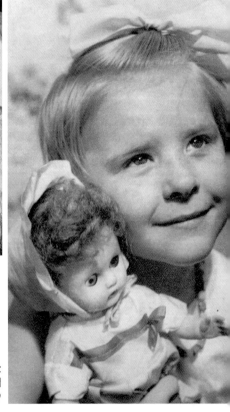

What A Doll: I don't look bad either, back in 1959

Head Start! My mum said: "Wear this — they will all have hats on." What a bloody liar, back in 1961

Like Mother, Like Daughter: My beautiful Sarah rehearsing for her role in the musical Annie

Three's Company:
A laugh a minute at
The Playhouse in 1986
when Micky Finn, me and
Pete Price, helped Brook-
side's John McArdle 'play'
a comic on stage

Pauline Daniels
Management:
Ricky McCabe Entertainments Ltd
Telephone: 051 920 3322

Pauline Daniels

Photograph
Paul Francis

Sole Representation:
Ricky McCabe Entertainments Ltd.,

My Publicity Smile:
February 1980. The
teeth and eyes have it

Bring It On: The Comedians in 1985. I took on the men and boys. I won

In the Middle of a Gag: Hello campers! Butlin's, 1983. I'm in mid-flight with sequins

Valentine's Day Again:
On tour with my favourite
alter ego – Willy Russell's
Shirley Valentine

A Saint She Ain't – Corinna Powelsland
(Martha Rae), me (Mae West),
Rae baker (Rita Hayworth)

SEE THE...
SWIRL
HERE TODAY

NEXT DEMONSTRATION

Brookside Babes: Well, we can
all dream can't we. A telly role I
loved for a while in 1990

Fellers, WARNING:
You wouldn't go home to her
with a fiver short in yer wage
packet. Me at The Everyman in
1986. I even scared myself

Red Hot Mamas:
Above, dress
rehearsal for my role
as Mama Morton
in 'Chicago', at the
Playhouse in 1986.
Below, Mama Rose
in 'Gypsy',
December, 1988

I sat down and talked with the family and, as usual, mum, dad and nan were supportive.

Dave didn't really care as long as he got his holiday and Sarah was only eight, so she was just glad to be going away and she was with her family so she would be fine.

The plus side was that the dog didn't have to go to the kennels so I'd saved some money, and we weren't going to lose any money on the holiday because nan's sister, Aunty Edna, would go in my place. Mum would sleep with her, Sarah would sleep with nan, and dad drew the short straw.

That time was really the demise of my first marriage. I'd got my wish and I was in showbiz, moving from the halls and clubs to theatres. Dave just couldn't cope because he thought that as I didn't need him to carry around my PA and have him working the sound for me, that I didn't need him. The truth was I needed him more than ever at that time but in a totally different way. I needed him at home looking after Sarah more, and I needed him to sort out his business. He had by now gone self-employed but because I was the main bread winner he didn't do every job that came his way.

We had gone through a financial crisis, but now I was doing a bit of telly – lots of stand-up, working most nights and he'd got used to being out late at night with me so getting up in the morning was a problem on its own. He also did love the horses and the pub a little bit more than he loved Sarah and me . . . apparently. But that, sadly, was the beginning of the end of Marriage Number One.

Rehearsals for 'Chicago' began and it was all strange to me, having to get up early and sing at ten o'clock in the morning – but I loved it. I was scared s***less on that first day. I hadn't acted since primary school in a French play and here I was with a load of 'West End Wendys', whose main job was musical theatre.

When we were introducing ourselves I distinctly remember the look of disdain from some members of the cast when I explained that I was a 'club act'. I felt pretty crap, but in a strange way it really spurred me on. I thought, 'I'll show you bloody lot, with your posh voices and wealth of experience'.

Three days in, the musical director arrived. Ian Kellgren was a fantastic lad whose roots were on the Wirral, so I felt I had a bit of an ally. Ian was great and he gave me so much confidence. When he asked me to get up and run through my number he gave a little wink, so I thought, 'what the hell' and I went for it.

Every one of the other actors in the room stopped dead in their tracks, their jaws dropped to their ankles and they just watched in utter disbelief. When I finished they all stood and applauded. From that day on I knew I was going to be able to do this and that they would now take me a little more seriously. I wasn't just a club act – I could be a musical theatre act, too.

All throughout rehearsals I was still doing the clubs. I had to – I was only earning £325 a week and I had a husband, a daughter, a home, two cars and a holiday to fund. As I was going round the clubs I was leaving leaflets to advertise 'Chicago' and I had a great following, so I really did hope that some of the people who came to the clubs would come to the theatre. They did.

My family went on their holiday and I was about to open in the biggest thing that had happened to me ever. All of a sudden, it struck me that all those people out there might have just come to see me die on my arse. What if I did? What if I forgot every word I had to say? What if I fell down the spiral staircase on which I made my entrance? What if my voice cracked? I was almost physically sick in a bucket.

When I went on stage they applauded so loudly that it took my breath away for a few seconds. I composed myself. I started my descent down the stairs and sang 'When you're Good to Mama'. The applause was deafening. I loved it and I was hooked.

I didn't have a walk down frock though. I had a grey skirt suit, cut to the waist and split to the thigh, a mink stole and stockings and all the time we were doing a dress rehearsal the wardrobe department had kept saying: "Oh, don't worry, you'll have a finale frock on opening night."

When I went up to my dressing room to get changed for the finale I was greeted by what can only be described as a red, white and blue shuttle. The American flag was draped from my arms at the back and I had a silver sequinned skull cap with the most amazing plumes in red white and blue. They must have been about two foot high.

Nobody saw the dress until the very last minute and when I went on stage to take my bow I felt like the Statue of Liberty in it. Of course, the chorus behind me weren't very happy because when they took their bow, no bugger could see them behind the feathers and the flag, but what the hell. It served them right for looking down their noses at the club act.

I went back to my dressing room, which I shared with two lovely ladies, Jacquie Toye and the most quintessential English woman I have ever known, Clovissa Newcombe. They were playing Roxie Hart and Velma Kelly, and we had become really good friends. They had even been to see me do my bit in the clubs and I had gained their respect.

Ian came round with notes – that's what a director does, because this was just the first night and things have to be ironed out before press night and we get thrown to the lions.

He said to me: "Well done, Pauline, you were fantastic. I only have one criticism: you don't need to come out like Rocky."

"I know," I said. There's no bingo or glass collectors.

They actually come to the theatre to be entertained. You don't have to fight, do you?

When everyone had gone from the dressing room I looked into the mirror and cried because, as a child, I wanted to do this. I cried because I had actually done it, despite not having any formal training, and I wept because I was all alone and everyone who mattered to me was in Greece.

When they all came home from their holiday I was an established actress. The press night had gone brilliantly and I stole all the reviews. The local papers in particular sounded proud to have me on their stage. They have been very supportive of my career ever since.

In 'Chicago', I worked with one of the most handsome men in showbusiness, a guy called Ricco Ross. What a name to go to bed with. He was absolutely gorgeous, but really quite shy. He was from LA and lived in Las Vegas. He had been in a few films including 'Aliens', so he had quite a pedigree. How cool is that? He was probably the first American I had ever met when I come to think of it. He looked fantastic and although I did sort of doubt that Billy Flynn – a lawyer in Chicago in the Twenties – would have ever been black, the way he looked took your mind off it.

He had to go to have singing lessons – he must have been cast in 'Chicago' by a woman. I mean, who else would have cast him in this – it was a bloody musical for God's sake!

I was broken-hearted when Chicago came to an end, but I now seriously had the bug and kept dropping hints that I really would love to play Mama Rose in 'Gypsy'.

I never thought for one moment they would take me seriously. After all, I was only 36, far too young to play the role that was created for Ethel Merman on Broadway and played so wonderfully by Rosalind Russell on film. Surely it wouldn't happen? But then I got the phone call and it did.

This was to be performed up to and over Christmas, my busiest time in the clubs. What the hell was I to do? Everything! So I did.

I would do eight performances of 'Gypsy' and then I would drive like the devil to North Wales and do a late-night spot in a cabaret hotel called The Springfield in North Wales. This is when I first realized I was in fact a workaholic. Yes readers – workaholic. I have been ever since – trust me.

I loved 'Chicago' but 'Gypsy' was something else. I revelled in the whole thing. I got to wear a wig for the first time, too, which wasn't so good. I've never been a big fan of wigs and if I can avoid them I will. I only ever wore one hairpiece which I adored but that's to come later on. In fact, the wig could have done a show on its own.

I met the cast on the first morning of rehearsal and there were two girls who had been in 'Chicago', so I didn't feel so left out of things this time. Also amongst the cast was the young lady who had let me use her dressing room at the Palladium – Danielle Carson, who was playing Louise.

The musical director was the same lovely Ian Kellgren who had done 'Chicago'. One night over a pint after rehearsals, Ian was telling me that the guy who played the part of Herbie had said he was worried I wasn't big enough. Herbie was quite tall and I am only five foot.

I used to be five foot and half an inch, but I lost half an inch somewhere. Anyway, he said I wasn't big enough, I was too hard and I wasn't old enough to play the role realistically.

Ian replied: "Firstly, Pauline will look older when she has a costume and a wig on. She's not hard enough yet and with regard to her being too small, I can assure you that when she hits that stage she will fill it so much, nobody will even notice you are there."

Herbie went bananas. I paid him back by having garlic bread delivered to my dressing room every interval. I'd discovered he hated garlic and it just so happened I had to kiss him in the second act.

After press night he was just as cruel. I had received rave reviews and he dismissed them as "Tomorrow's chip papers."

He really was getting up my nose, but I had a lovely cast so I didn't let him get to me too much.

On the last night I noticed that his black and white photograph had gone missing from the front of the theatre. it did cross my mind that some deranged idiot had nicked it but I didn't give it much thought after that.

Then hubby Dave and I had a blazing row. I went to bed in a stinking mood and put my hand under the pillow and, hey presto, there was Herbie's picture. I burst out laughing and we used that picture to quell arguments for quite some time.

They say you should never work with animals and kids. Well, 'Gypsy' had both those elements.

The animal in question was supposed to be a Pekinese but we auditioned and found a gorgeous little Shih Tzu. Joke: what's a Shih Tzu? It's a zoo without animals. Geddit? I know that's really crap, but it always makes me laugh.

Well, our little animal star was fantastic until the last night when, for some reason, he decided to run across the stage and cock his leg on a table at a completely bad time in the show.

The kids were from stage school and after working

with them I was so glad I never went. They were so pretentious. A few months ago I bumped into one of the kids. I don't even want to guess how old she was, but she made a belated apology. She was one of those kids who insisted on 'pulling focus' which sort of means that when something important is going on she was pissing about in the background.

I walked into the green room to catch the back end of a bit of a telling off she was getting from the lighting designer and as she and her friend were walking up the stairs, I heard her say: "God, you'd think it was her show."

Little bitch! Forgiven now though and after all that prima donna behaviour she got married, had loads of kids and dumped the profession.

After 'Gypsy' the straight roles came. I was honoured to be cast in an all-female version of a Trevor Griffith play called 'Comedians'. It had originally been done with stars like Jonathan Price and Jimmy Jewel and had been all men in the past but the Everyman and Kate Rowlands decided in 1986 that an all-woman cast would be groundbreaking.

The play was about a group of women who wanted to be comedians and they were being taught by an ex-comedian or, as in our case, comedienne.

The part had successfully been played by Jimmy Jewel but we had Anne Mitchell, a superb actress who had been in all sorts on telly, but had really been best known for playing Dolly in Lynda La Plante's great drama series 'Widows'.

I apologise to one of the two men who were in the

cast, because I don't remember his name, but he was Parker's voice in 'Thunderbirds' – now, that is real stardom!

TOP 5 SUPERSTITIONS

1. 'THE' SCOTTISH PLAY

Think about Shakespeare . . . one kid, at a show, kept on mentioning it, and, do you know, everything went wrong. He was the one who said M******. I broke my toe, people went off sick, fell over, you name it, they dropped like flies. And the lucky sod who said it in the first place – he was the only one left standing.

2. FEELING (UN)GREEN

I never wear GREEN. I once wore it at an Orange Lodge do and . . . I swear never ever again.

3. GO AND (NOT) WHISTLE

There's a thing about whistling in the dressing room – you don't do it. If you do, you have to go outside, turn around three times and swear. You get some funny looks outside the stage door. Such as a man with his wife pushing a pram. "Hey love, I just saw that Pauline Daniels swirling around three times and saying f*** off to no one. "She's lost the plot that girl."

4. DRESSING ROOM

I will always want the same dressing room in a theatre – the one I was in the last time I was there.

5. SHOES

In 'Blood Brothers', Willy Russell talks about putting brand new shoes on a table . . . it's traditional things that stay with me. I will always put my right shoe on first. I have always done it and always will. Touch wood!

DREAM REALITY
SHOW ROLE

STRICTLY COME DANCING
One of the great dreams of life would
have been to have danced with
the legendary Gene Kelly.

CHAPTER 7

Entertaining the Troops
(One at a time!)

"I have always been s***-scared of flying and now all of a sudden I had signed up to travel halfway round the world on a services 'dry' plane where you were not allowed alcohol and, believe you me, there is no duty free."

I WAS so proud to go and entertain the lads in the forces and my first trip took me to Belfast.

I had seen the way things were in Ireland on the television but nothing could have prepared me for the truth. It all began on arrival. As soon as I landed I was met by two men with guns and taken to my hotel, which was opposite Stormont.

The rest of the entertainment party arrived at the hotel and then we were all briefed by special police. This had now become bloody scary.

We went to our first gig in a vehicle that was almost a tank with no windows, just a small slit which went around the whole vehicle, and we were told that we were travelling through a Catholic township and it could be dangerous.

Whenever we stopped at traffic lights the soldiers in the passenger seats and at the back would jump out, rifles cocked. My bowels had started to relax slightly and this wasn't what I was expecting at all.

Travelling through the streets were a nightmare. On one side of the street boys on bikes – no problem. On the other side little girls with prams, no problem.

Well, not until they started firing missiles at us – milk bottles that were full of very small stones so that, hopefully, they would get through the small opening that was exposed.

We arrived at our first gig and as soon as I walked in two young soldiers came to me and asked could I take their mum's birthday present home for them as she lived close by to where I lived. They were just kids really, so young.

It was a great night and going back to the hotel we were assured that we were safe going home so we could go in a normal jeep. I sat inside the car waiting for the rest of the acts to join me and a young soldier put his head round and said: "Has anybody seen my rifle?"

I suddenly realized that whatever I was sitting on wasn't comfortable and, lo and behold, my arse was firmly planted on the weapon in question. Relaxed bowel . . . once again.

It was an experience I will never forget and I felt every possible emotion during that trip. We had to perform three shows a day. It's a bit strange when you go into a canteen at 11 in the morning – where they have drawn the curtains to keep out the light – and perform a whole show as if it was 11 at night.

Even stranger is the fact that your audience are camouflaged up in front of you and you are told not to worry if they all leave as they are all on 24-hour call.

The last night we were there we entertained the Black Watch lads and after the show the boys in the show were taken to the mess to have a meal with the lads, while I was taken to the officers' mess to eat a posh nosh with lead crystal glasses and silver service.

When the meal was over I think I offended the officers when I simply asked if it would be all right if I went and joined the lads.

They didn't seem to hold it against me, and they gave me a beautiful jumper with the Black Watch badge and a hackle (a feather plume) to take home as a souvenir.

The lads were so appreciative and I cried a few times

during that memorable trip. My emotions got the better of me. Two years ago I went back to Belfast and it was a totally different place – it's a wonderful city and it's so good to see.

My next trip out for the boys was the Falklands, well, after the conflict was over – a totally different experience to Belfast. I have always been s***-scared of flying and now all of a sudden I had signed up to travel halfway round the world on a services 'dry' plane, where you are not allowed alcohol and, believe you me, there is no duty free.

I knew that we were flying to the Ascension Islands and then re-fuelling before making our way to the Falklands. I was travelling with a good mate of mine, another comedian called Hal Nolan, along with Larry White the keyboard player, Steve the drummer and a strongman act. I was lucky as well because they allowed Dave to come along too – he went as a bit of a sound man for us.

We had one act with us who was a complete tosser (who shall remain nameless) but, you know, I don't think I've ever heard of him since anyway – God's good!

The plane took off and I had white knuckles. It was one of the scariest flights I had ever had. What I didn't know was that there was much worse to come.

We did land at the Ascension Islands and were on the tarmac for about an hour-and-a-half. They let us off for a drink of coffee (still no booze). The weather was fantastic and we were looking forward to being there on the way back, where we had two shows and three days' relaxation.

We boarded our plane again and the next thing I knew we touched down in this place that could have been the remotest part of the Highlands. It was bleak, to say the least.

The first thing we had to do was to don our survival suits – bright bloody orange. Mind you, we all looked ridiculous, and then we were loaded into a Wokka – that's the name the forces lads call the Chinook, because of the noise the twin blades make.

Hal had been driving us all mad all the way there about having been a soldier. He did his national service but he was beginning to sound like Liverpudlian comedian Derek Guyler in 'The Eric Sykes Show', when he used to go on and on about being a Desert Rat.

When he got into the Chinook we were all told that the pilot was on his last day – his nickname was the 'Red Baron' and he was going home, so we should expect anything.

My fear of flying was soon gone when I saw Hal's face turn a lovely shade of green. The back of the Chinook was open and this pilot couldn't get enough of flying just inches above buildings and trees. His speciality was to fly the helicopter on its side, which is a weird feeling when you look out of the back. I think that's when Hal threw up.

We arrived at our first base and we were met by a little Liverpool lad running out and yelling: "Alright, you lot, I'm in charge of the stores. We're all getting pissed – I've got the key!"

After the journey I had a drink which was just what I needed. The base was called Byron Heights and when we landed and took the survival suit off we realized it was bloody freezing. It felt like the strangest place in the world. You can get up in the morning and it can be beautiful with the sun shining and by the time you have got yourself dressed, the weather has changed and it's like the middle of winter.

We travelled everywhere by helicopter. This was not the sort of job I should have took with my fear of flying, but I was getting very used to it.

The war had been over for four years and everyone in the Falklands was just going through the motions. I have never seen so much food. Every base we went to fed us. It was getting so bad I was asking for meals off for good behaviour.

The alcohol was obscenely cheap. It was seven pence for a shot, so you had to ask for at least a triple. You could go to the bar and buy a round for 16 people plus ciggies and still get change.

You could also get very drunk in a very short time – perhaps that's why they all ate so much. I know an army is supposed to march on its stomach but, trust me, at four o'clock every afternoon, everything would stop for tea and sticky buns and there is no way you could even march back to your room for a lie down.

The shows were fabulous and the trips they took us on were fascinating. The rest of the show line-up was male and so you can imagine just what it was like to go and visit the fighter pilots and their big boys' toys – the lads loved it. The fighter pilots were very bored though, so they would just take the planes out for the fun of it.

Whenever a show would come out, they had a few female dancers as eye candy for the lads, and they would ask the girls to donate a piece of clothing, usually underwear. The fighter pilots would do the duty of passing them on and dropping them to the bases.

It seems daft but I suppose it was something to keep the lads' spirits up – and who was I to criticise them for it. I didn't give them any of my underwear for fear that 25 Argentineans might move into them and set up camp.

They used to sing a song, 'The Wokka Song', a very poignant number about how great those blades sound when you are making your final journey home and out of that godforsaken place.

It was bleak and very boring. In Port Stanley there were two prostitutes – just two, for all those troops. The poor girls. Their feet must have been killing them, up and down those stairs all day.

There were stories that when the planes all started to arrive on the islands the inhabitants were a bit put out. I am of course talking about the penguins. It was absolutely true that as the planes flew over, the penguins would follow them with their eyeline and fall over. Once they had fallen over, they couldn't get back up so the soldiers were actually on penguin duty. They went round, literally, picking up penguins.

On one of our days off we went and witnessed this. One of the lads had a great picture of Hal looking down at a penguin on its back and he drew a bubble coming from the penguin's mouth saying: "F*** off Hal, I've heard it".

That was a bad day for Hal. He had been boring us to death with all his army stories and about how he knew everything about everything.

The soldier taking us out that day came to me and said: "Listen, we have a bit of a surprise in store for Hal.

"We'll be travelling in a vehicle that is a jeep in the front and a sort of tank at the back." (Well, I'm a girl, he had to explain it to me that way.)

Now, we'd briefed the lads about how to sit in the back, as there is just one continuous seat that goes around the vehicle. However, we'd not told Hal, because apparently he knows everything anyway. "You'll sit up front in the jeep, but you'll be able to see the fun."

All the lads got in and waited for Hal, who was in his usual "I was in the Desert Rats, y'know" mood, so we couldn't wait to take off.

The terrain was awful and as soon as we hit the first bump, Hal came flying off the seat and just bounced around the back of the vehicle until we all stopped laughing long enough to stop being s***s and tell him how he should be sitting.

We had some very memorable days out. One time we were supposed to be going onto a warship and having a look around, and as we were just walking along the quayside a voice shouted: "Hey Pauline, I see you're on tonight – it was in the Echo."

It was a crew from Liverpool on a tug boat called the Indomitable. They talked our minders round and we were allowed to spend a day out at sea with them. We had a great minder. His name was Fitz, and he was SAS. He fascinated the lads with war stories but his job was to make sure we didn't come to any harm.

He had his job cut out too. We went on two helicopters that broke down, and on the only journey we made by road a wheel came off the jeep and rolled into a minefield.

On another occasion, just as were getting into the back of the Chinook, I discovered that my false nail – which was 9ct gold – had come off. Fitz rooted round in the mud for half-an-hour but to no avail. He didn't mind looking: it was a bit like Kate Adie losing her pearl earring when she was covering the war.

This day at sea on the Indomitable was a fairly easy one though. At first the lads on the tug wanted to show us an air-to-sea rescue and everything was set up for them to drop me into the ocean.

It was fine except if they were a semi second out my hands would have frozen and I could have even lost a finger. If I'd known that when I said yes I wouldn't have been so quick.

Anyway, the lads organised the right men for the job and the most dangerous thing I did was steer the boat for a bit and eat the food they'd prepared.

On the way home from the Falklands we got to spend three days of leisure on The Ascension Islands. We arrived at 11 at night and it was roasting hot. Nobody wanted to go to bed so we hit the fantastic swimming pool that was there. It was just so nice not to have to wrap up against the elements and wear that bloody orange suit.

The lads were in small, chalet-type buildings with bunks, but Dave and I had a really posh bungalow. The last guest there had been the Duke of Edinburgh. If it was good enough for Phil it was good enough for me.

We did two shows in the Town Hall and the soldiers took us out to fantastic beaches while we were there. We went shark fishing and to see the giant turtles.

Their eggs had hatched and the soldiers were taking the little tiny turtles down to the water's edge and virtually skimming them well out to sea because so many of them don't even reach the water due to predators.

In all we were out there for nearly three weeks and I had a fabulous time. There's not many jobs where you get to visit somewhere like the Falklands and get paid for it.

ALTERNATIVE CAREER CHOICE

I would have loved to have been a criminal psychologist. I fell in love with Robbie Coltrane in 'Cracker' and thought I could do that, getting in the minds of nutters. Later, I would do that with hecklers. By getting into other people's minds I could probably get into my own. I don't like the sight of blood so it's probably the best medically-associated career for me.

TOP 5 CHAT UP LINES FOR THE OVER 50S

1. Excuse me, but if that's your walking frame could I move it, sit down and chat?

2. Would you like to come to my place for a drink? It's alright, I've got two toilets.

3. Are you like me? When you bend down now do you go 'aaaaah!'
Great, we've got something in common.

4. How about . . . you and I going to the cataract clinic together?

5. Wouldn't it be lovely if our surgical stockings could share the same washing machine.

TOP 5 LITERARY LIKES

I have to be grabbed in the first few pages. If there are no blow jobs early on, I move on to another book! Current likes include:

1. JACKIE COLLINS – Lots of sex.

2. HAROLD ROBBINS – More sex.

3. ANGELS & DEMONS

4. JAMES PATTERSON – Crime novelist.

5. STAND UP & BE COUNTED – Me!

CHAPTER 8

Affairs of the Heart

"I had a daughter and in my mind she would be better off with her dad in her own home. Why should I drag her away from everything she knew?"

I REALLY should be against affairs. I mean, I have slagged off all of those footballers and, let's be honest, it's immoral and it hurts too many people.

So rather than do that, you should find out what's wrong with your marriage. If you can't fix it then get out, find a new man.

In 1985 I was having marital problems with husband Number ONE and I was working all over the country doing the holiday camps and having a pretty s***** and lonely time. As a gang in one of the camps we were all quite close, and there was a man that I was growing closer and closer to all the time. I was also pretty sure that he was fond of me.

So, would you believe, I went to ask my mate Ken, aka Paul Duval, what I should do about it. Picture the scene. One o'clock in the morning I knock on Paul's chalet, he lets me in. He sits on one bed in the dark, in his underpants. I sit on the other bed, fully-clothed.

I never even asked why we were in the dark but that didn't seem to matter. I had to tell him that my marriage was going tits up and that I had feelings for this other man. He was a sportsman and, at the time, quite famous – that's really all I need to say.

We sat in that cold, dark chalet while I poured my heart out to him and after about an hour in this dismal hut he said: "Have you got 50p?"

"What for?"

"The bloody electric meter. I'm f***ing freezing and if you haven't, all I can suggest is that you f*** off and sleep with him – so I can get warm again". Well that's what I did. So it's all HIS fault after all.

It was the start of a relationship. Well, no, it was an affair that went on for about 18 months on and off but I was getting nowhere at home and really wanted OUT.

I couldn't cope with it all though. I had a daughter and in my mind she would be better off with her dad in her own home. Why should I drag her away from everything she knew? I would be there as often as I could when I wasn't working. It would be okay.

I'd convinced myself that I could be at home for her when she got home from school and I could leave again when she went to bed and I would try and keep that up, which I did for about two weeks. I would ring her every night. I didn't know whether her dad had told her anything. I certainly knew she didn't need all my problems on her shoulders but I couldn't work the whole thing out.

I knew that after two weeks with this other man that it definitely wasn't him I wanted, lovely man though he was, but I wasn't a hundred per cent sure that it was Dave, either. But I knew I had to come home for my little girl. It all seems so long ago and yet while writing this it is every bit as painful now as it was at the time.

In the summer of 1999 I bumped into Ken in The Cheshire Oaks outlet village. I hadn't seen him for over seven years and I was on a break from the musical 'A Saint She Ain't', just before the transfer to the West End. We chatted for ages, about 40 minutes, and then went our separate ways.

Niggling in the back of my mind, was that there was something different about this man now. He had been my best mate for years and we had been through a great deal together. In fact, he saved my life once.

This year Ken and I celebrated our eighth wedding anniversary. We got married in Las Vegas. We weren't going to bother, but when we first got together we were together 24-7 and then I got a job at the Playhouse in 'Oliver' and I spent quite some time away from him in rehearsal.

It's true what they say: absence makes the heart grow fonder, and one night when I came home from work he just said: "I've been thinking, perhaps we should get married, but I'm not just walking over the road to the registry office. I want to do something different."

So we explored the options. The first was the Caribbean. Kenny had never been there and it seemed idyllic. I spoke to a few people, and they said: "Well, if you fancy a conveyor belt wedding then do it."

We toyed with the idea of Greece, God knows why, because neither of us had ever been there so there was no connection. Well, apart from my 'Shirley' connection but that's all. We found out that you had to be there so many days before, have everything translated back and forth from Greek to English and, to be honest, it was just a pain in the arse.

So one night we were discussing the idea and we thought, well, if it's a conveyor belt, it might as well be a total conveyor belt. Seeing as we were both from a showbusiness background, it might just as well be a showbiz conveyor belt. That left the very obvious choice of Las Vegas.

I actually said: "Why don't we have a drive-through wedding? After all, there's so much to do in Vegas you don't really want to waste much time getting married."

We decided against that, well, Ken said NO. We didn't have Elvis either. Well, we didn't need him, I had my own crooner. I didn't need anyone else.

We asked two friends to go with us – well, we asked one friend Mark and he brought his girlfriend, who was an out-and-out cow.

Mark was Ken's best man but I am being totally honest when I tell you we were just a bit skint. In fact, my cousin's husband loaned us the money to go and do the deed.

Mark's girlfriend knew exactly how skint we were and she went out of her way to buy the most expensive dress she could find for the wedding, knowing full well that I had just bought a simple jacket, trousers and top.

It was a lovely outfit but, to be honest, we spent more on Ken's suit. It was black velvet, with very subtle sparkles all over it. Yes, the groom looked lovelier than the bride – very Vegas – but I didn't care. I'd had wedding frocks before and they weren't that lucky, so what the hell.

The girlfriend continued to be a bitch, so much so that we started to avoid them. Actually, the truth is that we hid from them everywhere we went because, sadly, we were stuck with her for the whole trip which took us from Vegas to New Orleans, to Memphis, to Nashville, to New York.

My daughter said that we should have gone alone and got our witnesses off the street. That would have been interesting. Opposite the Little White Wedding Chapel is a string of tacky motels and sex shops so the only people we would have been able to get would have been hookers. That would have been quite cool actually, now I come to think about it, and we wouldn't have had to do all that hiding.

The girlfriend had bought a new state-of-the-art camera and said that she would do all the wedding photos. Would you believe she deleted them all by mistake? No, neither did we.

We managed to get three photos but they are lovely and the ceremony was beautiful, so much so that Ken and I both cried – not bad considering I'd had two previous ceremonies and they didn't touch me at all. We had a fabulous honeymoon, even on a shoestring. Ken fulfilled a dream of a lifetime. He recorded a couple of Elvis songs at the Sun Recording Studio – and I discovered that I did like Elvis after all.

Well, when I was a kid my mum loved him so I didn't. It's not cool to love who your mum loves, so I chose The Beatles, but I really did fall in love with 'The King' after going to Graceland and watching the 1968 comeback tour, over and over and over on the television in the Heartbreak Hotel. Well, come on, he must have been at his most handsome and definitely his sexiest in that black leather suit with that quiff falling over his face.

Oh behave, I'm getting all hot and bothered now.

Anyway, when we left Memphis and headed for New Orleans a little hurricane decided to come with us. I have never seen rain like it. We were sat in a restaurant on Bourbon Street having King-size shrimp and Jambalaya when the heavens opened.

People had to brush the water from the streets and

their shops. This was a baby hurricane, so when a few years later Katrina hit I could understand just how easily it had caused so much damage.

When it seemed the rain wasn't going to stop we went next door and bought one of those white rain poncho things. Kenny said I looked like a sperm. Nice.

And then I did what I always wanted to do. There was an overflowing drain and I just couldn't resist doing a 'Morecambe and Wise', in the sketch for 'Singing in the Rain'. I stood under it and then so did Ken. We were soaked through newlyweds and ecstatically happy.

We then drove from there to Nashville and Kenny did what he had always wanted to do. He had a super shirt, jeans and cowboy boots that he had brought with him. He bought a fabulous hat and we went to The Grand Ole Opry.

We finished the honeymoon off in one of our favourite places, New York. We had been there before, but this time we felt a little bit freer. The first time Ken went we stayed with his cousin Ann and her husband Gene and their two kids. One of the children looked like Bluto, Popeye's enemy. He greeted us one morning while we were having breakfast by walking into the kitchen grunting and inserting his hands down his pants and scratching his balls.

Before our visit, 'Bluto' had been to see his grandmother in Huyton in Liverpool and had held up the Post Office round the corner.

Obviously it didn't take long to find him. There weren't that many gun-toting Yanks in Huyton that week. He was put on a plane and sent home.

So here I was, miles away from home and living in a house with a ball-scratching, gun-wielding Bluto lookalike.

The family weren't drinkers and we were, so we used to get the train into Manhattan every day, buy some wine and whisky, or whatever, then at night we would take two glasses of water upstairs, empty the water, have a drink and then in the morning dispose of the empty bottles on the way out to Manhattan again.

Gene very kindly insisted that he picked us up from the station every night and we were starting to feel like prisoners, so one night I suggested we took a change of underwear, our passports and stay in Manhattan for the night. I thought I could get around Gene letting us stay out. I picked up a timetable for the trains to Great Neck and, brilliant, the last train was 12:05am.

I rang Gene at 12:10 to tell him we had missed the train but not to worry, we would stay in a hotel.

"What do you mean?" he said, "the trains run all through the night." I looked at the timetable, then turned the bloody thing over. S***, he was right. Not that we were ungrateful! It was kind of them to have us, but what a way to meet your new man's family.

On the last leg of our honeymoon journey, we went for one of our legendary wanders and stopped in Greenwich Village for a beer and a bite to eat.

We had two cold beers in chilled – well, almost frozen – glasses and we decided to go for the large Buffalo wings. I have never seen a plate piled so high.

Red Rum couldn't have jumped over this bugger. We were never going to eat these.

The guy in the restaurant packed them up in a bag and we walked back to our hotel on East 35th Street, completely oblivious to the fact that we were being followed by three dogs. The barbeque sauce was dripping from the bag and they were having a feast.

When I rang my mum, I told her what we were up to and that we were having some wings that we saved from lunch. She came off the phone and was worried to death. She said to dad: "God bless them, they must have run out of money, they are having leftovers for their tea." We were skint, she was right, but the best thing ever happened when we came back.

A friend of ours, Jimmy King, rang me and asked could I do a charity show for him on a Sunday in Cammell Laird's club in Birkenhead. Of course, I said yes.

Jimmy has done so much for charity over the years and taken it on himself to raise money for all sorts of tragic circumstances.

I remember doing a show for him years ago for a family of kids who lost their mum to cancer. He rang me Christmas morning and we were both in tears when he told me about the toys he had taken round and the joy he had witnessed.

The event he asked me to do was just after we came back from our wedding and honeymoon and Jimmy said that it was going to be filmed, so could I wear something suitable for an interview as well as the show.

Well, I had the perfect outfit – the suit I had got married in. I talked Kenny into wearing his suit – actually, Kenny never needed much encouragement to dress up. That's the showbiz in him.

We arrived at the club and were shocked to see it full to the brim and there were balloons everywhere, a massive wedding cake and all the family.

Our friends were all there and the entertainment was the best, all our mates. I did my bit – and can you believe, I still thought we were doing a charity show for someone until Jimmy got us both up on stage and gave us a cheque for £1000.

It was our wedding present from all the people in the club. They had all paid to get in, and I was so overcome, it was just one of the nicest things anyone had ever done for us. We are grateful for our good friends. We needed that money so much.

Ken was working in the day when we first got together and then doing the clubs at the weekend, so we weren't seeing enough of each other. I would go with him if he was working on a Sunday and I wasn't, and I could see how frustrated he was by the state of the game. He would arrive at a club that would be half empty and some little Hitler would say to him: "Set your gear up over there by the dart board."

All the lovely big cabaret rooms were closing and they were having their entertainment in lounges or games rooms. The audiences weren't there like they had been.

He hated the clubs and I hated going to work on my own, so we discussed it and decided it would be best if he packed it in and looked after me.

He had left his day job before. He was pushed out really. He worked for Barratt Homes as a sales negotiator but because he wasn't blonde with big boobs he wasn't flavour of the month.

They made his job difficult by moving him from site to site, making it impossible to see a sale through. Therefore he was unable of making any commission. So he got out.

You see, I thought women were the only people discriminated against, but 50-plus men with grey hair also suffer.

TOP 5 FOOTBALLING HEROES

1. BILL SHANKLY
The greatest manager of all time.
He was a very funny man. He was a tough,
gritty man who didn't suffer fools gladly.
He made Liverpool one of the greatest
football teams in the world. Also, he was
very much a man of the people – and a
Scotsman to boot.

2. JAMIE CARRAGHER
A good, honest Liverpool lad who gives
so much for charity. He cares about his
city and the underprivileged talented
kids who might not otherwise even get
to put a pair of football boots on.
His restaurant also cooks the best fillet
steaks in his home city (that should get
me a few freebies).

3. DAVIE HICKSON
Veteran star and for his uniqueness. He played
for all three Merseyside teams – Liverpool,
Tranmere Rovers and his beloved Everton.
A real gentleman.

4. DAVID GINOLA
Lovely hair. Enough said.

5. THE WHOLE 2011 BARCELONA TEAM
Lionel Messi is just the best player I have
ever seen in my life – pure class.

TOP 5 FOOTBALLING VILLAINS

1. GEORGE BEST
One of the greatest, most talented footballers of all time – and he threw it all away off the pitch.

2. WAYNE ROONEY
Come on lad. You've got a lovely wife, a beautiful baby and you spent some of your £250,000+ a week on prostitutes.

3. JOHN TERRY
How could you do that to your wife and your mate? Oh, hang on, there's been a bigger slime ball in football . . .

4. RYAN GIGGS
He did it to his wife, his brother, his mate, the butcher, the lollypop woman . . . no, I'm only joking about the lollypop woman and the butcher . . . I hope.

5. SIR ALEX FERGUSON
My most hated man in Footie. Okay, he's probably going to be regarded in history as the best football manager ever – but no self-respecting Liverpool fan is ever going to admit to that one.
Manchester United have a large number 19 outside Old Trafford at the time of going to press. Let's hope it stays that way. It's the number of league titles they've won. I say it's actually the number of times they touched the ball in the Champions League final against Barcelona in 2011. I loved that game and recorded it. I watch it time after time.

CHAPTER 9

Radio Daze

"I was a streetwise, funny lady who knew about football and music. Roger Phillips could tell you who was the leader of the most remote tribe in the world, but had no idea who the hell Oasis were. It was perfect."

IN 1995 I had just about had enough of travelling all over the country, blowing up car engines and running vehicles into the ground.

I was being interviewed on BBC Radio Merseyside and it just so happened that Ev Draper, who was second in command at the time, heard the interview.

She rang me and told me that there was going to be an opening "pretty soon", and she was interested in doing a pilot show to see how things worked out.

Her idea was to put me with Roger Phillips, who was well established as a radio presenter. He had been there for years and had won a Sony Gold award for his phone-in programmes and political interviews.

We were like chalk and cheese. I was a streetwise funny lady who was knowledgeable about football and music. Roger, on the other microphone, could tell you just about everything about politics, the NHS, the education system and who was the leader of the most remote tribe in the world. He had no idea who was the manager of Everton, Liverpool or who the hell Oasis were.

It was perfect. We disagreed on most things. He was, and still is, a great believer in the justice system and is all in favour of rehabilitation for criminals. I, on the other hand, either want them hanged or to lock them up and throw away the key. We started in March 1996 and I remember the first song we played: 'Wake Up Boo!' by The Boo Radleys.

Roger and I both lost loads of weight that year. Sylvia Lewis from the Macmillan nurses came in to plug a project they were involved in and it was 'DO

SOMETHING FOR A MILE', 'RUN A MILE', 'CYCLE A MILE' (you get the picture) – anything you could think of.

Roger and I were the least athletic people she had encountered. So Sylvia suggested we lost a mile's worth of fat. That sounds gross, doesn't it, but we both took up the gauntlet and I'm not sure how much Roger lost but I ended up going on to lose four stone. I felt great about it and we raised lots of money because we were sponsored by the listeners.

After divorce number two I lost another stone but I'm afraid that I have put on a stone since. I blame "the change" and "age" for that. Still, not bad in 14 years.

It was one of the hardest jobs I have ever had. Not the work; the getting up in the morning was a killer. I used to get up at 6am and then be in Liverpool at my desk at 8, ready to start at 8.30am. I was finished at midday and then I would have lunch and then set about putting together the next day's programme and then usually leave about three.

But in 1996 I was also doing other things. I was doing 'Shirley Valentine' at the Liverpool Playhouse in March and April, and then I was still doing holiday camps from June to September and travelling home every night. October was great. I was just doing the radio and local gigs as a stand-up. By November I was well settled and loving it all.

I loved being in the news room. It was always buzzing and I was there when a few significant things happened. The worst of them all was Princess Diana dying. There was a terrible cloud of gloom everywhere and it was very hard to get on with doing a normal programme for weeks.

Bill Kenwright rang me in Florida and asked me if I would do him a favour. He wanted me to do eight weeks of 'Shirley' – four weeks at Leatherhead Theatre, and then four weeks at Windsor.

He knew I was doing radio but he's no fool, he had it all worked out. I would do my programme until 12, then I would sort out the next day's stuff, then a driver would pick me up at one o'clock. We would drive to Leatherhead or Windsor, get there in enough time for me to grab something to eat, then do the performance. I wouldn't shower after the show (I put on a fake tan in the interval). I would get into the car at 10pm and by 1am I was in the bath at home and then in bed ready to be up at 6am for the next day. It was bloody knackering.

Roger Phillips and I became real mates and neither of us has forgotten the other's birthday to this day. We always see each other at events in the city and we always have a good laugh.

I was wondering one day why I actually really got on well with him, but on the other hand he could drive me round the twist. Then I discovered his birthday was the same as my first husband's – problem solved.

Roger and I had a fantastic producer, Lindsay Prosser, who was bloody mad. She would have the craziest ideas for guests and items for the show, but I loved her. She brought in a Big Issue seller one day. She just picked him up off the street and sat him next to me in the studio. Now, I'm sorry that he was homeless and there but for the grace of God and all that malarkey, but he bloody stunk.

I was in two minds interviewing schizophrenics – that was a bit scary, and even people suffering from Irritable Bowel Syndrome. Now, I suffer from that a bit myself (these days) but this poor woman kept ringing up to move the interview because she had the "runs".

Lindsay didn't care. If they were worth talking to she got them in. And, in all fairness, she was right to because we all need to be made aware of social and health problems.

They took Lindsay off our programme and gave her mainly serious things to do, which was good for her career, but our show was never the same without the weird and wacky guests she would provide for us.

I made a lot of friends on radio. My favourite period in the news room was that special time of the month for us girls. They say that if you work with a load of women it will eventually work out that you will all have your periods in and around the same time, and I can tell you first hand it is so very true.

Another great honour was to do 'Songs of Praise'. No, come on, stop laughing. I know what you're thinking and I'm telling you, you're not the only one.

When it was announced on radio that I was to sing a hymn live on Radio Merseyside the phones went mental. In fairness, mainly because people were genuinely pleased, but there were a few rather rude phone calls implying that we would all be struck by lightning if "that foul mouthed comedienne" uttered one note.

People can be so cruel. You wouldn't believe the

amount of people who ring the BBC to complain about everything, things that don't even involve the BBC.

I had a woman ring one day and ask how she was to get the pleats back into her skirt after she had washed it? I told her that I didn't know.

She was so s****y to me on the phone and said that I was the BBC and we were supposed to know everything. That's "what she paid her licence for". Trust me, this was one of the nicer calls.

Back to 'Songs of Praise', and the thought of singing 'How Great Thou Art' with the King's Regiment Band was so good. It took my mind completely off the fact that we were doing the show from Goodison Park.

The show was a two-hour special and I remember standing in front of all those people and thinking: "Well God, if you ever wanted to get me back for anything, here's your big chance. Take away my voice or, even worse, my memory."

But he didn't, and when I got back to the players' lounge there were so many people who said I brought tears to their eyes. They must have been singers.

I was also working at Merseyside when I was asked to sing at the Philharmonic Hall itself. The first time I'd performed with the orchestra was when I did Liverpool's Summer Pops Festival.

At 'The Phil', I had a fabulous band including my mates Paul Brookes, Mike Harvey and Gary Murphy. I answered the phone one day and Paul said: "Will you do something for me? Will you do a couple of numbers for me at the Phil?"

"Of course," says I. "What do you want me to do?"

"Who Wants to Live Forever, by Freddie Mercury and The Show Must Go On."

"You do mean the Leo Sayer one, don't you?"

"Oh, no love, the Freddie Mercury one."

S***!

"Of course, let me have a working backing track and I'll learn it."

"Great, you'll be on after the Opera Babes." Phone down. What the hell have I got myself into now? I had always been a Queen fan and, like everyone else, I can sing along to the songs on the radio in the car, but Jesus!

He was a clever b***ard that Freddie Mercury, and I cursed many a time when I had to learn that song, even during the performance, but it was a great success.

Not that I can tell you much about it. I was in a complete trance throughout the whole thing, semi-comatose, scared s***less and on another planet. I have never done drugs, well, only smoked a bit of stuff on a ship once, but never done the type of drugs that I could imagine would have put me in the same state as I was in that night.

Radio had its really good side, because I was still doing the clubs at night and so I was in touch with the people and knew what they thought about the programme and the station. It also meant I was needing agents less and less, because people knew where to get hold of me so I could handle all my own bookings.

That seemed like a brilliant idea, but when I came back from the West End it meant I had lost touch with everything club-related and things were tough.

Although I was happy in radio, the 'powers that be' had decided that it was time for me to go. There was a presenter working for the opposition and he had left, so the boss wanted him instead.

I was a little bit naughty the day I left. I had been looking for a song for a dedication and I was having a real good look in the library and I found this song. What a number.

I asked my producer and Roger whether they minded if I used it as my last sound off on the day I left. They were both quite happy about it, so I did just that. Strangely enough, people even to this day remember my leaving the station.

I know, I know, you want to know what the song was. Okay . . . but I'm telling you I suffered for doing it. Radio Merseyside didn't invite me to anything for about eight years, and my name was never mentioned in case the building should shudder and fall. It was by a man called Johnny Paycheck and the song was called 'Take this Job and Shove It'.

I was daft to do it, some say, but in general the public thought it was brilliant and I have never been the sort of person to just go quietly. Thankfully I have been forgiven and can even be heard back on those airwaves whenever some people go off on a holiday or whatever, and I really enjoy it.

My funniest Radio Merseyside experience was Christmas Night a few years ago. As you can imagine, not many people want to do the 10pm-1am at Christmas time, but my working life meant that it was a time that I was nearly always working.

It didn't and still doesn't bother me. So when I was asked to sit in I said, yes.

All went well, the evening was great and because it was Christmas, I got the chance to play people's requests and didn't have to stick completely to the music on the computer. At 1am I had to switch over to Radio Five Live, something you do every night. I had done it many times before and it had worked fine on Christmas Eve so I wasn't bothered by the idea.

It got to four minutes to, and I played what I thought was my last song. I said my goodnight – there are a great deal of people on their own at Christmas, and I had taken some pretty lonely phone calls.

I was on my own because nobody wants to work on production either at Christmas. There was just me and a security guard on the front door. I pressed all the right buttons, pushed up all the right sliders and guess what? No Five Live.

B***ocks.

I frantically searched through the computer and then, when the song was finished, I made my apologies and then played another song, and then another song, and then another song. 'Bohemian Rhapsody' was great, it's over five minutes long.

The normal security man Tommy rang me with a number in Manchester, I rang it . . . nothing. Nobody in Manchester wants to work at Christmas, either. The phones went mad, people were offering to bring me food – some people are lovely.

I was sweating profusely and thinking, 'my God, I'll still be here tomorrow when they do the breakfast programme and I will have played every bloody song on the sodding computer system!'

And then, at 1.40am, BINGO! Five Live appeared. I had sweated that much I swear I must have lost a stone. Scary, but very funny.

When I think back, the lad on the door, the security man, couldn't have given two s***s about me in that studio. It didn't even occur to him that I was a bit late leaving the place, but outside all the listeners were putting together food parcels and wondering how they could rescue me.

I've always loved doing the live shows at Christmas. One year I did an afternoon variety show for people over the age of 65. I pause to say 'pensioners' but, ok, I suppose that's what they are (do we have pensioners anymore?).

I had just helped myself to a cup of tea when this woman, aged about 68, came up to me and said: "It's terrible this, we have to get our own tea and help ourselves to our own bowl of Scouse (a famous Liverpudlian stew, too difficult to go into details now, but when cooked properly you can stand a spoon up in it). Then we have to take it back to our own seats. When we first came to one of these we were waited on, but now we have to do it all ourselves."

I replied: "When you first came there were 80 people in here, I know because I did the show and it was a gamble because they didn't know whether people would come. Now if you look around you'll see that it's stuffed. There has got to be 800 people in here, how the hell can they wait on everyone?"

"Well," she said. "It was better when it was empty, and another thing, the comedians seem to pay too much attention to one side of the room, and I can't carry my tea, I've got bad legs, hips and my eyesight is not so good."

I asked how much she had paid for her Scouse, mug of tea and three comedians and she told me it was £5.

I then said: "Well, I think you've got a cheek. Five quid for all that entertainment, food and drink and you're moaning because you have to carry your own stuff. I suggest you go home and bloody well stay there."

I know I shouldn't have said it, but I know so many senior citizens who are only too glad to have such things and don't expect the world to owe them a living. As she walked away, I said: "I don't suppose you'll be laughing when I'm on."

I was really pissed off and I thought, 'if that's the spirit of Christmas you can shove it', and then I went to St Vincent Blind school to read a prayer at their chapel.

Here was a group of kids, blind, some deaf and many badly disabled. They had collected glasses to send to the Third World and here they were thanking God for what they had and for being able to help others and I thought, 'I wish that moaning old cow from the afternoon event had been made to go with me', although somehow I don't suppose it would have stopped her complaining. I was so pleased I'd gone . . . at last the meaning of Christmas.

While I was working on the radio, I interviewed some really interesting people, including Paul O'Grady when he had just adopted Buster.

He was doing Cell Block H at the Empire and came in to just have a little chat.

I was in the studio one day when Mick Ord, the boss, came flying in and said: "Quick, get your coat on, Van Morrison is in the butty bar – see if you can get him to come in and do an interview."

The butty bar was where we all got our bacon, sausage and egg sandwiches for breakfast and, in Roger's case, every other type of food all day. I ran out in the pouring rain and into the butty bar and there was Van the Man at the counter.

"Excuse me, Mr Morrison," I said, "I'm from BBC Ra . . ." I never got to finish.

"F*** OFF!" he barked in my face.

I responded: "That will be a NO, then. You wouldn't like to come in next door and say a few words?" Miserable b***ard.

I mean, he might be a nice guy and maybe I got him on a bad day but I was pretty pissed off – and I got soaked. It was torrential rain outside.

That's not the only star to upset me.

Now this one's tough to relate, this really hurt. I was in London doing 'A Saint She Ain't' and I was going to the BBC at the top of Oxford Street to do an interview. I was waiting in the foyer and in through the door walked my hero . . . Sir Cliff Richard.

In front of me was the man I had idolised as a child – the man who I had avidly watched on the Eurovision Song Contest; the man who hadn't recorded a song that I didn't buy; the man who I had protected whenever people doubted his sexuality. . . the love of my life.

I was stunned when he approached me and then, with his right hand, physically moved me out of the way. I was distraught. I didn't know what to do. But I did want to shout: "Piss off, you bloody puff!"

MY DREAM DINNER GUESTS

1. BETTE DAVIS
One of the finest actresses I've had the pleasure of watching. She was one of the biggest bitches ever. I would love to have been able to ask her how she and Joan Crawford virtually killed each other. They fought over men, awards and roles. I'd have loved to have some insight into their story.

2. HYLDA BAKER
She was a pioneer for women in comedy. Her father had a troupe of players – and she was one of them. She was only a kid when he was hit on the head by a sandbag in the theatre, and died. She got everyone together and trundled this troupe around the country, and she made her name through determination. The sad thing is that there weren't many people at her funeral. She died a sad and lonely woman. But she had a soft spot for men. I would love to have talked to her about that.

3. MARGARET THATCHER
I can't deny that I don't have admiration for her because she did what I never thought I would see – becoming our first woman PM. She made mistakes, sadly to the demise of the poor working man and woman.

She brought us through the Falklands War and the people there had admiration for her. But, sadly, when it comes to coal mines and most other manufacturing services, she was the beginning of a lot of our problems.
But she'd have so many great tales to tell.

4. BESSIE BRADDOCK
She was a total champion for housing, for birth control, for everything – and obviously for Liverpool – for making the city great. She made mistakes – she joined the Communist Party – but she realised her mistakes and got out when she did. I bet if you stopped a man in the street in Liverpool and asked him to name his top five Scousers, she'd be there along with Ken Dodd.

5. MAE WEST
My ultimate heroine. Four foot ten inches, with eight inch heels, which explains her swagger. She discovered Cary Grant and is responsible for some of the best one-liners ever. The original 'Tart with a Heart'!

CHAPTER 10

West End Girl

"I was an overnight star after
20 years of flogging my arse
up and down the country,
entertaining the masses."

IT was 1999. I had decided that I was really loving the acting side of my career and I would love to do more and go a bit further afield.

I also thought that I was fairly stable in my personal life – I had divorced Dave and remarried.

I married Husband Number Two (spit) for all the wrong reasons. Oh, I had better explain, spitting is what I always do, if I ever have to mention him that is. But I have to be honest – I try to avoid it at all costs.

People ask me now why I married John, but I defy any woman not to have. He bought me a house, a car, gave me cash, and a place to escape from the marriage that I was desperately unhappy in.

It was working fine until he kept badgering me to marry him. I eventually broke and agreed in 1993.

We had moved to a bigger house and he had commandeered the car that he bought for me, so really here I was, married to a man who, I'm sorry, I just didn't love. I now had nothing. The house was in his name and I had to ask to borrow what had been my own car.

I was too busy working to worry too much about it though and I was determined to get a big job. I went to see Sara Randall, the Grand Dame of the theatre world, and we agreed that I would let her represent me.

I left her office and went to the famous Joe Allan's restaurant in Covent Garden, a place where all the arty farty famous go for lunch.

I hadn't been there half an hour and Sara rang me. She had got me an audition with Ned Sherrin for a new musical called 'A Saint She Ain't' and the part they wanted me for was Faye Bogle, who was a parody of Mae West.

What an opportunity. It was the week later on a Sunday morning when husband number two drove me.

I had a backing track of 'Frankie and Johnny' and a tape player, in case they didn't have one, and my music for 'If they Could See Me Now' from 'Sweet Charity'.

I wore a calf length black dress and I borrowed a long cardigan from Sarah that had ostrich feathers round it.

Oh, and high heels. I'm always scared of someone saying "She's too small".

I went into the building and I was told to wait for a while. There were young girls waiting, but nobody my age, so I felt quite confident, although Sara had told me that they had already seen a number of 'name' actresses.

I was focused, I wanted this and I was going to get it.

Of course, I haven't told you the downside of all this. It was to be performed at The Kings Head in Islington, a theatre/pub that held about 120 people. The fee was a pound a head, £120 a week.

How the hell could I live off that? I would have to find somewhere to live and pay rent and eat. Oh shit.

I was called into the main room with what seemed like a massive panel of people, including writers Dennis King and Dick Vosburgh. Of course, nobody knew who the hell I was because, to be perfectly honest, if you don't live within the London Bubble they don't think you exist. Well, not in this business they don't, and boy oh boy, do they forget you as quickly?

I gave my music to Chris on the piano and sang my

first song. They seemed suitably impressed, but then I insisted on shoving my Mae West as far down their bloody throats as I could.

I had come a long way to do this audition and I wasn't leaving until I was happy that I had given it my best shot. I sang my 'Frankie and Johnny' and they loved it.

Then they gave me a small section of the script which I read with Dick Vosburgh. They laughed – well, that's always a good sign.

I knew I had done a good job. I went home and waited, and waited, and waited . . . it seemed like months. Oh, wait, it was months, three to be precise, but then came the phone call and I had got the job.

I later found out that Dick and Dennis had decided as soon as I left the room that I was the one they wanted. Ned on the other hand wanted a 'name' and so carried on looking for a while, until he had to give in and agree that there was only one woman for the job.

Now the real hard work started. I had to find somewhere to live.

I only knew a few people in London and had to see if anyone had a room that I could have for three months, for very little money – because I didn't have any.

What chance did I have? I was actually the luckiest bitch in town, because a friend of a friend had a flat she needed looking after for three months while she went to Scotland to look after her Mum, who was a bit poorly. It was in Golders Green, a bit of a bugger on a Saturday if you wanted to go shopping, but a lovely area and on the right tube line for the Angel Islington.

I moved in on the Sunday, ready to start rehearsals on

the Monday. I had given up smoking on 31 December, 1998 and so I had now been a non-smoker for three months.

It was the beginning of March 1999 and I was stood outside a rehearsal room in London. I was, in fact, metaphorically shitting myself.

There was a little shop next door so I ordered a cup of tea and 20 Marlborough Lights. They were the first packet I could see, and I smoked about four or five before I went into the rehearsals. I was so scared of what I was about to walk into I had now become a smoker once again.

I walked into that room and recognised all the people who were there at my audition, as well as Barry Cryer.

I remembered him from game shows when I was younger. I didn't recognise anyone else, but they all knew each other and, again, I was the odd one out.

It was just like when I did Chicago all those years ago, only this time I was 44 and I had a wealth of experience behind me. Surely that would make a difference?

Did it bollocks. I was just as scared. I introduced myself and told the truth, that although I was an actress, I was really just a club act – a stand-up comic.

They didn't seem too bothered, but they certainly weren't impressed. I had been in this position before with actors and I knew that once I did my big number they would love me, and they did. I grew to love all of them and we were a lovely tight-knit company.

On my way home from rehearsals one night Sara, my agent, rang me to tell me the good/bad news.

The show was to transfer to the West End, at The

Apollo, Shaftesbury Avenue. That was the good news.

The bad news, however, was that it wasn't a done deal that I would go with it, as they were again hoping to put a name into the role. I told Sara there and then that it wouldn't happen. I said: "I am going to be so bloody good at this, that nobody, no matter how big a name they are, will be able to follow me".

I had never meant anything so much in my life and I was determined that when this show moved, I was going with it.

The Kings Head was a fabulous place and I loved it all. Everybody who was anybody went there and worked there.

Of course, everyone in showbusiness knew Barry, Dennis, Dick and Ned, so everybody came to see the show and I met so many famous people.

During rehearsals, I was able to get a freebie ticket to go and see 'Jeffery Barnard is Unwell', starring Peter O'Toole. I was blown away. It was a masterclass in acting and I sat through this jaw-dropping experience knowing I was witnessing one of our greatest actors in full flow.

I had totally fallen in love with Peter O'Toole, even though he was about 64. His eyes twinkled and I had been lost in them from the moment he walked on stage.

He was the finest actor I had ever seen and I used that performance as a yard stick from that day on.

You might wonder why I am telling you all this? As I said, everybody came to see the play, and Barry Cryer introduced me to the world's greatest in those three months. I met Dave Allen, Victoria Wood, Thora Hird,

Ronnie Corbett, Michael Palin, Tim Brooke-Taylor, Andrew Sachs. Oh, and Nicholas Parsons. Well, not EVERYBODY who came was a superstar.

Actually, I remember a particualr incident with Andrew Sachs.

I had just arrived at the Kings Head with my mum and dad for a Sunday afternoon performance and we were in the front bar. Barry was there talking to Andrew and he introduced me to him. He half turned and gave me a very dismissive look, grunted and then turned away.

After the show, he came up to me and was quite gushing about my performance. I grunted, gave him a dismissive look and turned my back.

If you can't be bothered to meet somebody and be nice, whoever they are, don't bother when you decide that you want to know them. Fawlty Towers has never been the same to me since . . .

On the night that Thora Hird came to see the show, she was celebrating a birthday. I can't really remember which one, but she was in her eighties, and after the show that night they put on a little buffet and drink.

I came out of the dressing room and there was my idol – the great Peter O'Toole.

Barry said: "Come on I'll introduce you."

I said: "It's okay, I'll do it myself."

I thrust my hand out to be shaken and he held my head in his hands and said: "You were fantastic."

Then he kissed my forehead, my chin and my cheeks.

I just turned in a daze and said to Barry: "Lawrence of Arabia has just snogged my face, I'm going home."

Sadly, I didn't get a photograph, I was too stunned

that this genius had not only kissed my face, but really thought I was good. It remains one of my greatest moments ever.

While I remember, I must tell you the story about when I met Robert De Niro. I was in between husbands at the time and Number Two (spit) had said to me: "Pack a few things, we are going away for a few days. Bring your passport."

I got to Manchester Airport to discover I was going to New York and staying at The Waldorf Astoria.

(Are you beginning to see why I married this man in the end?)

We checked in and were upgraded to the Tower. I was now staying in a suite bigger than my house, with a dining room, sitting room, a bedroom and two bathrooms. It was massive. I had never seen a bed that big. Great – I wouldn't have to sleep too close to him.

When it was suggested we go for dinner at the Tribeca Grill, I suggested that lunch would be better – I knew that Robert De Niro had a production company in the building and if he was in town he was more likely to be there in the day time. Bingo. I was only right wasn't I?

We arrived and ordered and we were sat in a sort of booth.

Husband Number Two (in waiting) said: "Don't look now but there's a fella behind you who looks like Robert De Niro."

What happens when someone says: "Don't look now"? Yes, the first thing you do is look.

I did and it was my hero. He was sat at a table talking to an elderly man with flowing grey hair. They were

Ma, if you could see me now…Oh, you have: A special 70th birthday celebration at the Apollo

ad and Me:
ys it all. On holiday with
e favourite feller in 1986

Coming up Roses:
Backstage at the King's Head, London, waiting for my big entrance in 'Gypsy'

Educating Pauline:
The proudest moment of my life, being honoured by John Moores University for my contribution to the arts in 2009

Fame: In a bar in Ibiza. I had become a gay icon in 2004

Queen of the Comedy Festival: 1993 at St George's Hall. I've always felt like a Queen. I'm just glad I haven't got the real one's children!

School's Out:
Mark Moraghan, star
of Brookside and
Holby City is a great
pal. We both relished
being part of Willy
Russell's musical 'Our
Day Out' at the Royal
Court in August 2010

Making wavelengths:
Getting up early
wasn't easy every
morning, but working
with broadcaster
Roger Phillips was a
joy. I never shut up on
the radio back in 1996

Absent Friends: Left, my great panto chum Jeremy Beadle, who was always game for a laugh. Above, the legendary Sir Norman Wisdom

Sir Kenneth Dodd just said:
"Have you been using bad language again, you strumpet?"

2006: Lily Centre girls in the pink

Shirley Valentine: Royal Court, 2010. I can always count on Shirley to get me rave reviews

Starting out in the 80s: On a wing and a prayer. If the jokes didn't work – I could always sing!

Betty with a gob on: Willy Russell's classic 'Breezeblock Park' in 2002

Tony Brown 100 Heads:
Proud to be one of this great artist's collection.
My life with cuttings, personal photos and a
montage of everything I've done (sort of)

harassed by all sorts wanting autographs, so they moved into a back room. I then went on a reconnaissance mission just to check whether there was any exit from that room without passing me. Hoorah – there was no way out!

We ate our lunch and had another bottle of wine, but still no sign of the master. I wanted to tell Robert De Niro that I had admired his work and how wonderful an actor I thought he was.

Another bottle of wine came to the table and as it was getting close to the bottom, he appeared.

I turned and as he walked past my table, I tugged on his trouser leg, and when he looked down at me I said: "Hiya, I think you're great!"

He looked at me with a very puzzled look on his face and then said: "Oh hi. Thanks."

That was it, my great speech to one of the finest actors of our time. What a knobhead am I? I went back to my hotel and drunkenly rang my mate Ruby and said: "I'm in New York, I've just seen Robert De Niro!"

"F*** off" she said, and slammed the phone down. I'd forgotten about time differences.

Back to the story though . . .

After the Kings Head and The West End is when I bumped into Kenny again after seven years. I made a big mess of everything and we nearly didn't manage to get together at all.

I was so pissed off with Husband Number Two, I almost had a bit of a fling with a lovely young lad called Les. The trouble was, he was just that TOO young.

He was in his twenties and was infatuated with me,

bless him. I was a good girl, but I could have been naughty. If that was today, and I had taken it any further, I would have been called a Cougar. Apparently, that's a woman in her fifties who sleeps with boys younger than thirty. I know!

I couldn't be arsed. I was chatting the other day about this with a woman in the pub and she said she's a MILF, which is apparently Mother I'd Like to F***.

It gets worse – there's also a GILF. Yes, you've guessed it. A Grandmother . . .

I know. Mind you, to be honest, there are a lot of beautiful women in their sixties and seventies these days, but I just can't seem to get my head around this at all.

The really sad thing about lovely Les is that after I left London, he and his mates were out one night on the razz and he was run over on Piccadilly and he died. Such a waste. He was a talented lad and I really enjoyed his company. Who knows, maybe in another life, eh?

Actually, I had a period of time when I seemed to attract young men. I think that after listening to me they must have thought, "Bloody hell, this woman knows her stuff, I might be able to learn something here."

Sadly, I have never been attracted to the younger man. They never seem to have anything worthwhile to say.

Anyway, when we moved to The Apollo, even more stars came to see the show. The opening night was amazing.

I was so pleased to see three mates there; Roger Phillips and Sheila Fogarty from Radio Merseyside, and my mate and fellow actress Eithne Browne.

When I did my big number, 'The Banana for My Pie', the theatre stopped. The applause was the most deafening and it seemed like forever before we could carry on. During that applause, Ethy turned to the people behind her and said: "That's my mate."

Later, one of the reviews said that my Banana song had more double entendres than the whole of the 1940s put together.

The aftershow party was amazing. Roger Moore, Twiggy, Robert Powell – all the stars that had come to the Kings Head.

Roger Phillips sat in a corner and ate, nothing new there then. Ethy and I ended up in some club or other. I have no idea where, but the next morning I had a card in my handbag with the name of a Baron on it.

I could vaguely remember drinking champagne, buckets of it, and I knew we hadn't bought it. This Baron must have, but I never did get the nerve to ring and find out exactly who he was. It was the best ever first night party that I had ever had and I knew the show was a success and so was I.

Everybody kept asking where I had been hiding myself. I was an overnight star after 20 years of flogging my arse up and down the country entertaining the masses.

I was invited to all sorts of parties. I went to one with my lovely Colin Cattle and when I sat down, a bottle of champagne arrived for me from 'a fan'. Paul O'Grady got to his feet as I arrived and shouted: "Ladies and Gentlemen, the toast of the West End, Pauline Daniels."

I had arrived.

I had a membership for Grouchos and would go with Barry Cryer. Because I had second billing, I was important. I didn't realise this, but when Sara my agent was doing the deal, she rang me and said that they weren't offering enough money. Then she rang to say that they had agreed the money but she was fighting for second billing.

I told her I didn't care if I was one up from the effing printers, I wanted the job. But she explained that when you are in the West End, your billing and dressing room number is important, and unless you are one or two, you can forget it. God she was so right.

All invitations that came to the theatre were for me and Barry. I used to love it at the end of a show. There was always a mass of people for autographs.

Everyone else in the cast looked the same off-stage as they did on-stage, but I was a totally different kettle of fish. I was padded out, I had very high heels, a wig to die for – platinum blonde with ringlets – and an American accent.

When I walked out of the stage door, I was five foot nothing, short blonde hair, with a Scouse accent that would say: "Shall I get them in Barry?" and then I'd sneak into the pub and get the ale before last orders.

All the time this is going on you will have noticed that there is no sign of Husband Number Two. He always used to say that it was a bit of a drag for me to come home and then go back again, and it was difficult for him to drive down, so it was best really if I stayed in London as much as possible.

I didn't mind. In fact, I didn't care. I had friends there

and Colin was always working in London, so whenever I could, I would catch up with him.

Colin invited me to the Royal Albert Hall one Sunday night for a gig he was doing. Emma, his girlfriend – now his lovely wife – met me with my ticket and I was led to a box, right opposite the stage.

I was stunned when I saw the programme on my seat was for the Stonewall Concert. There on the bill was Elton John, George Michael and conducting the orchestra (he always said, "on the stick") was my mate Colin Cattle. The show started. Jimmy Sommerville and Madeleine Bell came out on stage and I just looked up, saw Colin and started to cry. Oh my God, the last time he and I had worked together was in Pontins in Southport and just look at us. He's on the stick at the Royal Albert Hall and I am starring in the West End. It couldn't get any better than that.

Well, actually, it did – there was a party afterwards and George Michael said he had seen me and thought I was great. Wow, that man is gorgeous, I mean really gorgeous. Just a midge's dick away from Patrick Duffy, who still remains the most handsome man I have ever seen in my life.

I was rubbing shoulders with the most famous people. Paul Gambaccini commented on how great he thought the show was. Sandi Toksvig, Graham Norton, Paul O'Grady, and then I met the master, Elton John himself.

I have to admit he was lovely, surrounded by bodyguards, but very nice to me all the same.

If Husband Number Two had known I was going to be in that kind of company, he would have broken his back to have been there. He was, how shall I put it now, a bit of a social climber, to say the least.

However, this was the back end of the marriage and, by this time, he had moved on to a bigger fish.

Well, he thought he had and he actually thought he had got away with it, but that's another story. It's a bloody good one though, girls.

Anyway, I was in the throws of having a great time and being toasted by the great and the good in London's West End and loving it.

I was on my way to Grouchos one night and I passed a lad begging on the street. In his Scouse accent he said: "Have you got fifty quid for a cup of coffee love?"

I stopped and laughed and said: "If I had fifty quid, lad I'd give it to you!"

We then had a chat about Liverpool. He asked me what I was doing, and so I got him a ticket for the show. I know he came down because I checked with the box office.

We Scousers do tend to stick together like shit to a blanket, even though I'm only a semi-skilled one.

One night after the show, all the cast wanted to go to the Arts Club but they were all moaning because you had to be a member and none of us were.

Of course, I wasn't going to be refused. "Come on, I'll get you in", I said.

I didn't have a clue what I was going to say, but I knocked on the door and waited for the man to open the little slider to see who was waiting to come in.

He slid it across, but before I could say anything, he screamed in a raving queen way: "Oh my God, it's

Pauline Daniels! I used to watch you at Butlins when I worked there years ago!"

We all got in and we all got memberships. So you see, I would never knock working at holiday camps.

You never know where people are going to turn up and when you'll need them. And they need you.

On a roll with a little honey

FIRST NIGHT:
The nostalgia
musical *A Saint
She Ain't* tickles
**Benedict
Nightingale**'s
fancy

Pun people: Mae West (Pauline Daniels) and W.C. Fields (Barry Cryer) successfully import *A Saint She Ain't* from the King's Head to the West End

s Mae West almost
asked, is that a pun
in your pocket or are
you pleased to see
me? Certainly the answer offered by this delightful spoof
of 1940s Hollywood musicals
is yes, and yes again. Puns,
quips, double-entendres, mal-
apropisms and jolly repartee
seem to come pouring out of
every part of the stage, from
the palm trees to (yes) the characters' pockets, and the feeling
is so ebulliently welcoming we
found ourselves helplessly
chortling at what we might
have snuffily dismissed as
Christmas-cracker silliness.

The programme says that
Dick Vosburgh and Denis
King have based their show
fat the Apollo on Molière's *Imaginary Cuckold*, a play unfa-
miliar to me and, I suspect, to
Molière himself. Still, the al-
leged debt allows Andrews Sister lookalikes to bounce on,
singing that if the great
Frenchman had gone to Hollywood "I know he'd be raking
in the dough". That blend of
earthy fun and sly sophistica-
tion typifies what follows. Imagine Cole Porter contributing
to a collaboration between
Groucho Marx and Irving Ber-
lin, and you have some of the
rhymes and much of the feel.

My expectations, I admit,
were less high. Perky musicals
that succeed in a friendly pub
theatre — and this comes from
the King's Head — can look a
bit limpet in the West End.
Moreover, I wasn't hugely tak-
en with the idea of bringing on
characters evoking West, W.C.
Fields, Jimmy Durante, Abbott and Costello, Rita Hayworth and Gene Kelly to perform a sentimental romp
about sailors in town. It sounded nostalgic and irritatingly
knowing. It sounded a pain.

Well, nostalgic it is, but a
pain it isn't, thanks to Ned
Sherrin's refusal to let his production get excessively self-par-
odying, to King's period
hums, and, above all, to Vosburgh's unstoppable words.
The plot is predictably prepos-
terous. Barry Cryer, alias Sina-
veley T. Bogle, alias a squint-
ing, saturnine Fields, is married to Pauline Daniels, alias a
Mae West who majestically
wiggles about in dresses that
make her look like a lazy Brad-
ley or a vast rococo raspber-
ry. Gavin Lee's tap-dancing
Danny decides Fields has commandeered his fiancée, Rae
Baker's gorgeous, flame-
maned Anna. West draws
some wrong conclusions, too
— and so to a dénouement as
flimsy as tinted celluloid.

But this matters not at all
when Brian Greene's confused
Durante is declaring himself
on the horns of a Dalai Lama,
or Vincent Marziello and
Michael Roberts's Abbot and
Costello launch into yet anoth-

er wonderfully goofy routine,
or someone is accusing Fields
of being two-faced and someone else answering that "if he
had two faces, why would he
be wearing that one?" Nowa-
days you are not meant to
crack jokes about people's
looks, still less their alcohol-
ism or nymphomania: but
when the show has a go at sex-
mad West or at tipsy Fields, I
found it wickedly refreshing.

She sings a splendidly ro-
bust song about Danny being
the frankfurter in her bun, the
banana in her pie, the organ in
her chapel, and invites him to
her room for a late breakfast
consisting of "just a roll with a
little honey". He cracks lugu-
brious jokes about the evils of
the demons water and milk,
threatens to annihilate an enemy by breathing on him, and
attributes his permanent hang-
over to "getting a bad piece of
ice". Did we laugh? You bet we
did.

THEATRE
Scenes From An Execution
Barbican Pit

Jeremy Kingston

A HIT when first staged at
the Almeida in 1985, with
Glenda Jackson as its fierce
heroine, and previously a
prize-winning radio play,
Howard Barker's strong,
whirling drama is now
revived, directed by Barker
himself, with Kathryn
Hunter as its thrilling
centrepiece.

Ostensibly set in
16th-century Venice, but
sparkling with throwaway
allusions to the present day,
the painter Galactia is
commissioned to cover a
thousand feet of canvas with
the Battle of Lepanto, only to
outrage the authorities by
revealing the gory, screaming
reality of war in place of its
mythical nobility. In casting

doubt on the glory of
self-sacrifice she is seen to be
criticising the state, nay,
Christianity itself, and flung
into prison. Release comes
accompanied by a string of
ironies, the last of which
emerges when Galactia, after
just one further glance at her
work, accepts an invitation to
dine with the Doge.

Barker famously walks his
own, often isolated, course
through modern drama.
Were it not for the Wrestling
School, the group of actors
and designers formed ten
years ago to focus on his
work, we might never have
seen his *Ursula* last year, that
luminous exploration of
marriage and virginity. Nor
perhaps this production,
vividly presenting the
inevitable conflicts between
lying politics and visionary
truth, between the demand of
the artist and the command
of the State.

On a central rostrum,
where a dripping canvas
(from a painting? from a
galley?) is repeatedly hauled
out of water, Hunter's
Galactia sketches a sailor for
his wounded belly, an
Albanian Muslim for his
head, her lover (James Clyde)
for his buttocks. The play's
arresting opening is her
observation, "Dead men float
with their arses in the air,"
and it is just this sort of
unheroic detail that has
made her a danger to a State
bent on glory.

Hunter's performance is
outstanding, gazing upon the
simpler folk around her with
lustrous eyes, flashing her
quick and flirty smile. Her
limbs, hips, all her joints,
shoulders, elbows, neck
ripple as if even the energy of
her voice and her author's
imagery are not enough to
convey her teeming feelings.
Her voice darts, booms,

clangs with the power of
someone determined not to
make her own will
subservient to the wills of
others.

The play's reliance on a
structure of two speakers at a
time reveals its radio origin,
but this matters not a scrap
when dialogue is as bracing
as this: subtle, witty and
dangerous. Tomas Leipzig's
theatrical equivalent of
long-shot and close-up, the
eye, and the company's
performances offer a range
of different excitements: Ian
Pepperell's Doge, urbane
and panicky, Gerrard
McArthur's elusive,
hectoring Admiral, the
dangerously thoughtful
Cardinal (Alan Perrin) and a
lively performance by Julia
Tarnoky as Galactia's prim
and pettish daughter.

"As Mae West almost asked, is that a pun in your
pocket or are you pleased to see me? Certainly
the answer offered by this delightful spoof of 1940s
Hollywood musicals is yes, and yes again."
A review of 'A Saint She Ain't' from The Times, 1999.

EMBARRASSING MOMENTS

"I have a morbid fear of coming out of the loo
with my frock tucked inside my knickers.
I remember once delivering a punchline on stage
and ended up doing an impromptu splits on the
slippery floor."

CHAPTER 11

Shirley and Me

"Shirley had a very big
influence on my personal life.
For once, I realised that
I had the rights to an opinion
and to change things."

WHEN a script falls through your letter box it always holds a great deal of excitement, but the day 'Shirley Valentine' dropped on my mat I was struck for the first time in my career by pure fear.

It seemed so thick so, erm, full of words and so . . . just me! What the hell had I agreed to? I'd never learn this in a month of Sundays. Too late now though – I'd already agreed to do it.

I suppose being a stand-up was a great help, in the fact that I was used to being there all alone on a stage. But that was different – that was me. If I cocked up they were MY words. I could wriggle out of it, well, to a certain extent, but this was different; this was somebody else's words. This was theatre – no room for ad-libbing here.

B******s, what had I done?

I couldn't start early enough trying to learn this script so I decided that the best way to do it would be to recite it into a Dictaphone. For about a month solid, I walked around with this little machine and headphones attached to me. I even went to sleep with the headphones on! I cooked, cleaned, ate, drank, bathed. Everything I did I was attached to 'Shirley'.

By the time I came to rehearse I was, as far as I was concerned, pretty damn close to knowing it all. That, of course, went completely out of the window on the first day of rehearsals. Nerves got the better of me and it seemed like I didn't know a bloody word of it.

I had heard rumours that several well-known actresses had agreed to do the piece, but after seeing the script had just pulled out due to the volume of learning involved. In fact, one actress in particular just said nothing, then didn't turn up to rehearsals.

When they tried to get hold of her, they were told that she had simply left the country with her boyfriend, Brian May. Oops, you know who it was now. I can't blame her, but OMG, (that's me getting down with the kids) what a fool. She robbed herself of the best script ever.

After a day or two it was fine – it was all coming back. All that work was worth it. But as well as learning all these words I had to be two dimensional and cook a meal on stage.

I had to peel potatoes, wash them, chip them, cook them and then fry two perfect eggs. I never broke a single yolk. All of my husbands would say: "Why couldn't you do that at home?"

When the chips were down I responded. My chips were a perfect shade too. These had to be precision-timed, there was a certain amount of dialogue and by the time I reached the end those chips and eggs had to be perfect.

I have never failed to date (fingers crossed). I did a charity performance and spotted early on that the stage crew hadn't switched the cooker on at the mains, so I spent the first 10 minutes of the play trying to work out how I was going to bend down at the back of my kitchen to switch the bloody thing on.

I managed to hide it as I pretended to pick up all sorts of imaginary things off the floor. I am, in actual fact, brilliantly perfect when it comes to egg and chips, but my culinary skills end there.

I was doing a whirlwind tour of the country, a week here, a week there, and I loved every minute. But I also found it very difficult being away from home for so long. I had been travelling quite a bit on my own up to now, but this seemed different.

I was staying in digs, which can be very lonely. As much as I could, I would share with one or more of the other girls. I had a team of four: a company manager, a wardrobe mistress, a stage manager and an understudy, who also doubled up on stage management.

When you are on your own you get too much time to think, and Shirley was starting to have a BIG effect on me. My marriage hadn't been ideal for quite a while, but now I could stand back and take a good, long look at what was going wrong. I seemed to be more and more like the character I was portraying every day.

I rang my bessie mate, Colin Cattle, when I was in Canterbury, and asked him to trek over and stay the night so that I could use him as a sounding board for my problems. We spent the night drinking and talking and I did a lot of crying, but in the morning I knew that it was the end of my marriage.

It was very hard to go on stage that night, but as I always say to anybody who is starting out on an acting career, use your negatives and turn them into positives. If you're hurting, use it in your performance, and I did, so much so that in the first act, when Shirley talks about a time when her and Joe "used to laugh a lot with each other" it hit home so hard that I couldn't hold back the tears.

Strangely enough, it still is a hard section to do without

genuinely filling up and recalling the good times of my first marriage.

There were never any major problems on tour, but one Monday I was on my way to Wakefield and I hit the most horrendous traffic on the M62. There was no way off the motorway and I was well and truly stuck.

I rang home and asked Dave if there was anything he could suggest I do, like as if he could help! I sat in that traffic for half-an-hour and then rang Dave and screamed at him to make it right. Poor man, what could he do? He had called the theatre and couldn't get an answer, it was the box office and an answer-machine.

I was sweating and really worried. First night, new town, show starting at 7.30. It was now 6.30 and I am a good half-an-hour away and I hadn't been there before, so I had to find the place – no satellite navigation then. I love my Sat Nav now. Up until getting that I had a man in the passenger seat with a map . . . more of a 't*** nav' really.

Dave rang me to inform me he had phoned the local police and they had gone and knocked the stage door down to let them know where I was and approximately how long I would be, so they decided to hold the curtain. I arrived at 24 minutes past 7, the curtain went up at 7.34 . . . what a pro!

Professional girl, not a prozzie.

God, I was scared though. Now you would think that a close call like that would be bad enough but later that night, whilst sat at my on-stage breakfast bar peeling my spuds, one of the metal legs fell off the set and rolled down the rake of the stage and into the pit.

I know I said that you can't ad lib in a piece of theatre, but there comes a time when you have to address something like that, otherwise the audience are just all thinking about the piece of set that has fallen off the stage. I just looked as it rolled away and said: "That's the last time I shop at MFI."

In 1996, at The Liverpool Playhouse, I was struggling with a parasol in the last act, about five minutes from the end. It just wouldn't open.

I carried on with my dialogue and I was coming to a section about Joe arriving, so I said: "I've got tonight off though, well, Joe's arriving tonight. I hope he can fix this bloody umberella."

The audience will always appreciate it when you can do that and they like it when things go wrong. We are a sadistic lot.

They were the only two set problems I had until 2009 at The Royal Court in Liverpool. I was about 20 minutes in, with 800 people in the audience, and I leant on my worktop and it totally collapsed. Unfortunately, as I was leaning on it, I couldn't help but fall. There was an awful clatter and then a lot of blood and then gasps from the audience.

They brought the curtain in. They wanted to cancel the show, but I said: "No, just find out where this blood is coming from, get me a clean pair of tights and we'll carry on."

I'd fallen on a glass and the knife I was peeling potatoes with, so a very sharp knife. It had cut my wrist just shy of my artery and the blood was pumping out, and my legs had little cuts from the glass. I went to the dressing room, sorted myself out with plasters and new tights and it took a total of 21 minutes for them to make the set safe. The curtain rose to an amazing ovation. I got a lump in my throat, but then said: "Anyway . . ." and the audience burst into laughter and we carried on.

I say WE – I mean Shirley and ME of course.

I did the whole play and everything was fantastic, a standing ovation, it couldn't have been better. I got home and then it hit me. Now I know what delayed reaction really is. I shook and cried for an hour. After that, I never went on without having some big lad stand on the worktop to make sure it was safe every night.

While I was on tour I did once do something unforgiveable and totally unprofessional. You are not allowed to stay or go more than 25 miles away from the theatre, for obvious reasons. Justine (wardrobe mistress) and I often nipped off for the day.

When we were in Basildon she talked me in to going to London to see Jason Donovan in 'Joseph and His Amazing Technicolour Dreamcoat'. I went in kicking and screaming but came out wanting my daughter to marry him. Then back to Shirley.

That was ok, but the day we did something very naughty was when we were in Canterbury. We decided we would nip over to France for the day. We had discovered it was something like 24.7 miles away from the theatre but we thought it best not to tell Ray, the company manager, or Sue, the stage manager. She was a bit of a snitch.

Anyway, off we went and we had a fabulous day and then when we got to the Hoverport. They said that the weather had changed and that they might not be able to get us back.

We were in a place called Deep S***.

We didn't know what to do. We just sat there with everything crossed and thankfully we were fine. We made it back with time to spare. It was to be our little secret – nobody need ever know.

It sounds fine in theory. Soft bitches us though had bought the company some cakes, from a French patisserie with the name all over the bloody box.

We received a stiff b******ing, but Ray was lovely. He never put it in the show report so Bill Kenwright never found out . . . well, not until now anyway! Bill, I'll send you a signed copy of the book and some croissants.

I never really thought about this until writing this book, but Shirley had a very big influence on my personal life. For once I realised that I had the rights to an opinion and to change things.

I didn't have to settle for a boring life indoors. I was a person in my own right and although I have made personal mistakes since doing the play, for the first time I do subconsciously ask myself: "What would Shirley do?" In fact, since Shirley, I really have found my own voice and become myself.

Although sometimes I stick with things because it seems the easiest option – anything for a quiet life – I do eventually "wake up" and discover that there's a better life out there and it may mean facing life on your own and being a little lonely at times. But, it's better to be lonely on your own than be lonely with someone else.

Thank you Willy Russell – you helped me find myself and I am well on my way to becoming that butterfly.

Shirley the best yet

A SHIRLEY Valentine was in the bar before the show; a Shirley Valentine was also sitting in front of me. But there on stage was *THE* Shirley Valentine.

Pauline Daniels has moulded the one-woman play in such a way that we hang on every one of Willy Russell's words.

And what words. Ten years to the day it was first performed and the modern classic just gets better.

Pauline is no stranger to the role and it shows that when it comes to delivery she is in a league of her own. One moment a facial expression turns her into a bored schoolgirl, the next a grumpy Scouse accent creates husband Joe.

Wandering around an excellent kitchen set or a sun-kissed island rock, thanks to designer Bruno Santini, we are given all we need by the Playhouse production team to join Shirley as she shares secrets about her need to enjoy life ... again.

For those who haven't seen a stage version, make this the one.

Granted you have to work a little harder than in a cinema but with a guide such as Pauline the magical mystery tour of self-discovery is a sheer joy from the time we see her making real egg and chips to when we finally leave her.

Theatre is all about imagination

By Peter Grant

and Willy Russell's work, in the hands of a craftswoman such as Pauline, offers the audience the chance to paint its own pictures of characters and situations we can all relate to.

When Pauline is telling a tale about a school nativity play her timing is impeccable, just as it is when she sips from a glass of white wine and savours melancholy thoughts on what might have been; the silence is deafening.

Shirley Valentine, a decade old and in Liverpool again with Beatles music as a whimsical backdrop — what a homecoming.

And as for Pauline Daniels, she is absolutely grace ... honest to God.

 STAR RATING:
★ ★ ★ ★ ★Pure silk

Celebrating ten years of Shirley Valentine with a performance at The Playhouse, Liverpool, in 1997. Ooh look, it's the editor of this book, Peter Grant! I've aged better than he has ...

"There is no better Shirley Valentine than
Liverpool's very own Pauline Daniels."
It doesn't get better than that, in your hometown.
A review from the Liverpool ECHO in 2005.

Pauline stands up to mid-life crisis

Review

SHIRLEY VALENTINE
Everyman
JOE RILEY

TWENTY years on, the stretch marks barely show on Willy Russell's masterful analysis of female revolt against domestic chores.

But perhaps the mid-life crisis has moved on? Perhaps if he were writing this wondrous monologue today, Shirley would be 52 rather than 42.

Whatever, all the ingredients are in place to ensure a rollercoaster of emotion.

And there is no better Shirley Valentine in my experience than Liverpool's very own Pauline Daniels.

Daniels was the first Scouse stand-up comedienne to conquer TV.

Since then she has made a truly remarkable transition into legit theatre, tackling narrative and musicals with equal distinction.

The trio of Valentine performances she is reprising for this year's comedy festival (also tonight and tomorrow) are truly remarkable.

With such a versatile and commanding actress at the helm, suddenly one realises how

Shirley is a close relation to Russell's Rita.

Both had a flawed schooling, from which they are determined to move on.

In Shirley's case, she is also moving on from a stagnant and abusive marriage.

One positively wants to hug this woman as she makes the break – and that grabbing emotion is down not only to the skill of the writing, but also to Daniels's epic performance.

All the cameos – from husband, headmistress, class bully, next door neighbour, to Greek lover – come easily from her much practiced comic repertoire of impersonation.

The best of these, in a full-on music hall sort of way, is the Manc at the Mediterranean beach bar.

"Marriage is like the middle east. There is no solution," muses Shirley talking in confidence to her kitchen wall.

The splicing of unrelenting reality with dashes of fantasy is a Willy Russell hallmark.

Ultimately, his characters do move on – but with the aid of an 80% back story.

In this case, both the writer and the actress are retained gems of Liverpool talent.

It makes me proud to write about them, which is more than can be said for most of today's ragamuffin one-dimensional stage usurpers.

Acting is about range. It is not about sameness.

As such, Pauline Daniels both delights and surprises.

And that's what true entertainment is all about.

RATING:

10/10 Top notch

181

CHAPTER 12

The Tragical History Tour

"A comedian just stands there and bares his or her soul. It's not down to whether the crowd like anyone, but you. And if they don't, well, you can be in serious trouble."

DON'T fall over in Bournemouth. There's nobody there strong enough to pick you up. It's the only place in the country where the shop 'Next' is an undertakers.

I am joking, of course.

Actually, the more I think about that – the truer it is.

Hal Nolan was based there for the summer, and the show he was doing was 'Summertime Special'. He was staying in an apartment, and I wrote him a letter (there's nothing better than your mates congratulating you on your success, so I wrote saying I thought he was great and did a really good job).

The letter he wrote back is one I still have, and when feeling as miserable as a box of dead sparrows, it always makes me smile. He wrote:

Dear Miss Daniels,

Mr Nolan thanks you kindly for your comments. Obviously, an act of his magnitude is unable to reply to all his fan mail and so I, as his secretary, have great pleasure in doing the job for him.

He hopes you will be a fan for some time and continue to watch his career climb. Please find enclosed a signed photograph of Mr Nolan on his balcony and thank you, yet again.

Yours sincerely,

Mr Nolan's personal secretary and assistant

The paper was a bit of foolscap pulled out of a book, with ragged edges and the writing was in blue Biro. The photograph was hysterical. It was Hal leaning against a balcony with a cigarette in his hand, held between thumb and second finger, and almost down to the filter. It always makes me laugh. But then Hal always made me laugh.

A few years previous we were working together on a pilot TV programme which was a bit like 'Punchlines'.

You know, half the gag was told and then the teams would finish it off. I wish I had a copy of that tape. (actually, has anyone out there got one? I sound like Billy Roberts, the psychic).

Hal was, now let me see . . . 'alternative', before alternative was the fashion. We stayed in a hotel adjoined to the Nottingham Royal theatre and we were recording at Central TV.

We had Duggie Brown, Tom Pepper, Hal in the back and myself in the front of a cab on our way to the studio. Hal just never shut up, but was very funny.

He said to the driver: "Hello there, mate, you probably recognize myself – Hal Nolan, from TV's, 'The Comedians', 'Summertime Special' and many other TV appearances. And on my left, Duggie Brown, one of the original 'Comedians' from Granada, who did the classic joke: 'I'm the plumber, I've come to mend your pipes'. The young man on my right, Tom Pepper, a rising star, who was in 'Live from Her Majesty's' and is about to become a panel game host, and the girl here . . . SHE just travels with us."

Ta, Hal.

In the bar of an evening, he was the same. One night, these two guys came in, one in a check shirt and the other in a cream jumper. He said: "Good day boys, how did the cricket match and barn dance go?"

It was always a bit of a cover though. All the comics seemed to be friendly, but deep down inside they were very insecure and vulnerable.

I could never ever understand why these extremely shy men all wanted to unzip themselves in front of a room full of strangers, to be picked at, sometimes until there was no flesh left on the bones.

When you are a singer you need to have a fairly good voice, because the public don't let you get away with anything easily. But if your voice is in tune you'll get by because it always comes down to the songs you sing. For instance, if a male singer was struggling, all he really has to do is sing a Michael Buble song and he'll win his audience back.

It's not the same with a comedian. He or she just stands there and bares his or her soul. If they don't like your material, you can be in serious trouble. It's a lonely life.

I didn't believe that in the early days because I had Dave with me all the time, but as soon as he stopped coming with me I began to discover it to be true. If you have a bad night, who can you tell? No one. You are just left to stew in your own juice all the way home and then nobody is up, so you start to have a few drinks to wind down. I can also see why comedians very often become heavy drinkers. Thank God for the menopause. I just can't drink that much anymore.

Bloody hell, I never thought I'd thank the menopause for anything . . .

I'm not one of those manic depressive comedians. What you see is what you get with me. I don't think I am any different as a person on stage or off, but I know a few who are. I also know a few comics who have to WORK at being funny.

I could never understand that. I always thought that naturally funny people would be the ones to choose a career in comedy, but there are quite a few who are, let's say, bloody miserable off stage.

I love the naturally funny ones: Micky Finn and Tom O'Connor. Micky's act has always been observational, which is what popular comedy is today. Doddy loves him, so you can't get better reviews. I think he's funnier today than ever, and his son is now following in his footsteps. See, I told you this is a lonely life – laughter is everything at the end.

Many years ago my great mate Colin Cattle and I had a special code for people who were out and out 'prats'. His lovely mum, long passed now, was a Pratt before she married her Charlie, and she used to say: "I'm one of the Pratts of York." A cracking woman who left her mark on me.

Whenever Colin and I had met a REAL prat, we would just look at each other and say he or she is "ON THE BUS." We had this idea that we would put all the dickheads on a coach from here to Australia. So, remembering the passenger list I have built up over the years, here's a journey that you wouldn't want a ticket for.

Husband Number Two is obviously driving the bus. This would put the s***s up anyone. He was one of the worst drivers I have ever had the misfortune to be in a car with, although I do have a funny recollection (just one) about him in a vehicle. When you get a chipped windscreen it's disastrous.

But when the sun roof goes . . . Well, his became bigger because he was too mean to get it fixed – so he thought he'd be clever and put a bit of plastic over it in case it rained. In theory not a bad idea.

In practice . . . hysterical. It was after the terrible Christmas of 1999. The atmosphere all over the holiday had been awful.

He was now driving me back to London to work, and taking dad and mum with us to celebrate her 70th birthday.

He locked up the house and we were all in the car. Nobody gave a thought to the fact that it had been raining the night before and so we took off.

As we turned a corner, we discovered the plastic sheet over the sun roof must have had a hole in it.

I wish I could say I'd done it (snigger, tee hee) but, honestly, I hadn't. The obvious happened, – the rain water poured through, and he got well and truly soaked.

Hubby Number Two had his sense of humour removed at birth. Of course, on that journey I couldn't hold my laughter in but mum and dad stifled everything as we watched this utter 'knob' dripping from head to toe.

It wasn't the best start to a trip, but it kept me amused all the way back. He didn't even start to dry out till Birmingham.

My first husband Dave would make a great bus conductor.

He's chirpy enough to annoy everyone all the way to Sydney, and he really is only happy when he's got money in his pocket and a roof over his head (not a dodgy sun roof), no matter whose it is. I'd make sure he's got enough ale to be even more annoying.

That would be the crew.

Now for the passengers.

All of those people who have upset me have the dubious pride of place.

ACTORS

Quite a few of them – especially the ones who think they can act and despite pulling the wool over the public's eyes. They stand out like a sore thumb to those of us who know.

I always thought that comedians made good actors. If you look at the likes of Max Wall and Russ Abbott, I'm sure you'd agree that they have a knack of being able to perform with immaculate timing.

No, not all comics can do it. So, to all of you who think you're Laurence Olivier and insist on criticising other actors . . . **get on the bus**.

In my career, actors who are prima donnas want the 'Number One' dressing room and the like.

They have 'riders' (the dressing room demands for flowers, drinks, food, etc) in their contracts for ridiculous things that they don't need and really don't want, but they think it makes them special.

Well it doesn't . . . **get on the bus**.

To be fair, it's not just actors who do that. Performers of all types have this obsession with surrounding themselves with things they don't even have at home, just because they can.

AGEING ROCKERS

Particularly Sixties pop stars who refuse to go grey. They dye their hair within a millimetre of its life so that they end up with three Shredded Wheat on their heads instead of being themselves. What are they frightened of? Their hair may be black and not move in the wind but their necks do! **Grow old gracefully**.

HAIRDRESSERS AND CHEFS

Those who think they are celebrities – **get out of the faces of truly talented performers**.

AGENTS

There are some right sharks out there. Girls, if you are thinking of starting out in this business be very careful.

There are those who will rip you off and continue to bite the hand that feeds them. Remember, they work for YOU . . . it's not the other way around.

There were two agents in Scotland who would offer you a week's work for a set fee and it would comprise of picking up your money or, as we say, "no pick ups".

This is the bit you never want to get involved with, because when you worked for these guys in Scotland and the North East you would find that, very often, you had picked up your total wage by Wednesday.

You would never know what they were charging the venues after that for your fee. They would be pocketing the remainder. Trust me, they would pick up more than you ever did. There really are some awful agents out there who will stop at nothing to trick you and rip you off. We have a few here in my home town.

I'd say there are two fellas and a woman that I wouldn't trust as far as I could throw them. Well, there's a couple of seats for the men, but as for the woman, I'd be happy if you stood all the way.

PLASTIC SCOUSERS

They do nothing at all to endear any of us to the rest of the country, and most of them have lived away from Liverpool longer than they actually lived here.

And we all know that the accent is so heavily put on that it's a joke in itself. Behave yourselves, we're not daft. You can all go on the top deck, along with theatrical kids and their mothers – now!

YOUNG PERFORMERS

I'll be totally honest, I loved working with all those kids on Willy Russell's 'Our Day Out', except for one of them. Now he will know who he is actually. So will all the other kids. The cheeky bugger tried to direct ME on my third day of rehearsal and then went on to cock-up everything he did on and off stage.

DAMIEN, take a seat.

AND ONE MORE SEAT WITH NO CIGAR

I wrote to 'Jim'll Fix It' once. I wanted to be in Hadleigh's dining room with Gerald Harper: he at one end of his extremely long dining table, and me at the other, and all I wanted to do was say: "Pass the salt please, James." It never happened.

Then I wanted to lay on a chaise longue, in a tiger-print gown, with a cigarette holder, and have Bryan

Ferry sing: 'These Foolish Things Remind Me Of You.' That didn't happen, either.

So, for that reason, I'm putting Jimmy Saville on the bus.

OTHER COMEDIANS

Those who spend their lives telling you what a great night they had last night and how they: "Did a bomb, tore the b******s off the place, did a stormer." Apparently they never die on their arses. Well, they're all liars, and in most cases they haven't worked a club for years.

They all go off to Spain or go on cruises, mainly because they can't get work in their home town anymore. Stop lying and sit behind the Plastic Scousers.

The passenger list is full now – they know who they are. If you are reading this in a shop and haven't bought the book, you are on the bus as well.

But should we meet, all it will take is a large brandy and I promise I will tell all . . .

Enjoy the ride all of you – DING DING!

WOMEN DRIVERS

"I have never thought of myself as a lady driver or woman driver. Once, at Butlin's, I was fuming about women drivers after I had just had a brush with one. Everyone fell about laughing.
See, I really am one of the boys.
But it's true, I don't fit into that man-made categorisation of women drivers. I don't – and won't – consider myself one.
After that Butlin's remark, I went outside and climbed into my car. I was doing 40,000 miles a year on the road for six, sometimes seven nights a week at this point, always in the car. Anyway, I went outside and reversed straight into a wall with everyone watching. I never lived that one down."

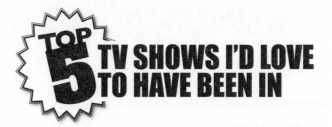

TOP 5 TV SHOWS I'D LOVE TO HAVE BEEN IN

1. DESPERATE HOUSEWIVES
No, not Gobby Scousewives. It's entertaining.
Isn't all telly? It's well written and glamorous.

2. DALLAS
I'd love to have been offered a part in the
original or the re-make. The shoulder pads,
ranches, JR . . . I can dream.

3. PRIME SUSPECT
I'd love to have been in something like this,
playing a really strong, female detective.

4. CORONATION STREET
In the days of Elsie Tanner and Ena Sharples.

5. DINNER LADIES
Fabulously written for women.

WHAT WOULD YOU CHANGE ABOUT YOURSELF?

"I'd never have any cosmetic surgery, but I'd love to put my legs on 'The Rack' and stretch them. Oh, for long legs!"

CHAPTER 13

My Art on my Sleeve

"Usually, when I come on stage, I can see and smell the fear of the men in the room, especially if they're too close to you."

FOR the stand-up show I like to see the audience. If it's a theatre, I like to somehow get a look at them as they're coming in.

If it's a club then I will stand at the bar and observe. I have to be there at least an hour before I go on just to do that. In a theatre, I would probably stand out front and have a fag just to observe.

You will get little pockets of people who you'll think: they're going to be trouble unless I get stuck in first – either because they've been on the ale, or you know they are going to heckle. So I'll look for that. It's probably my number one thing. I'll then look for men who maybe look like someone – who have a resemblance to anyone famous.

I always like to have a hand-held mike. I don't have a wire – I like to be able to wander all over the place, which freaks the f*** out of them.

There's many a time when I have followed the odd man into the toilet with the mike. I will also check on anyone who looks a little bit wimpy or weak.

They usually sit at the front because they have to . . . everyone else is sitting at the back first.

Usually, when I come on stage, I can see and smell the fear of the men in the room, especially if they're too close to you. And then they realise that it doesn't matter how far away from me they are – I'll get them. So that's how I prepare for a stand-up.

I like to see the people. All my material is international because it's mainly about life, and women and men in general. I sometimes throw in the odd topical gag but what's the use of using something that happened ages ago – it's no use. I will find out where the posh part of the town or city is wherever I'm appearing – because there will be a gag I can do about a posh woman. So I will find out what their equivalent is to the Wirral's Heswall. But then I'll do that if I'm working in Crosby. I'll talk about nearby Blundellsands. I tailor that anyway.

I'll also find out the rough areas – but I don't really do any gags like that. I'm very much a down-to-earth working-class woman who never really goes for cheap stabs at places like Cantril Farm or Kirkby.

I've never really done that. I don't see much point. I'd rather take the piss out of the posh place. If I've ever got anyone in from Heswall – I'll always ask (if there is) – you'll get the odd person who will put their hand up and I'll tell them to just sit back and hear what YOU sound like. But they take it well – they're fine.

I don't do politics and, apart from my Pope gag (sorry, you won't hear it in this book, you have to come and pay to see me, but I'll sign the book), I don't touch religion. And the Pope gag's not anti-Catholic; it's anti-hairdresser. So I would never change the Pope gag because it's about a Scouse hairdresser. It doesn't matter where you are in the world, the minute you put on that really heavy Scouse accent everybody laughs.

I do Cardinals as well. I was in Cardinal Heenan School once, and I said something like "the devil was in me that night". Well, it was some fella with a red hat on! I looked up and saw a picture of the Cardinal on the wall, and said it might have been him. All the audience completely pissed themselves laughing, and then I realised it was Cardinal Heenan and I apologised but they all just thought it was funny. God bless me.

I did a Catholic club in Kirkby and I said to somebody: "I don't do many Catholic clubs, for obvious reasons." Then I went and stood at the bar and there was a fella there and he said, in a lovely Irish accent: "That was fabulous that – I really enjoyed the Pope gag." So I said, "Oh, good." And he said, ". . . I'm Father (whatever his name was)." A real priest – and a fan.

I did another Catholic club and I was halfway through the night and someone said the priest was there. So I went over to him and said: "Are you the priest?"

He said: "Yes", and I said: "So where's the dog collar?"

That's a lousy trick to do to me – not to give me a clue. I'm not a Catholic, but I respect everybody else's rights to believe in what they believe in. I've never been biased towards religion or anything really.

So that's not really my bag. A lot of my act is about ME growing up, being a teenager, going through puberty, going through pregnancy, going through marriage, and marriage, and marriage.

And now going through the menopause.

And going through the loss of a parent.

In between all that there are odd one-liners and gags that fit in, and my grand finale is the Pope gag. No matter how many times I try to drop it and find something else, someone will always say they brought their mate to hear that.

You know, whenever we're rehearsing a play and we've had a bad rehearsal, I always say, 'don't worry about it, I'll do the Pope gag, and Pearl's a singer, and we can all f*** off home.'

I mentioned at the start of this book I would talk about nuns. No, it wasn't a clerical error. It's nothing like 'Sound of Music' or the 1959 classic film starring Audrey Hepburn and Peter Finch.

This really happened to me, and rates as one of the toughest shows I have ever done. It was not a habit I was going to get into. Right, that's enough nun jokes, I must confess. We'll have nun of that . . .

I was booked for a posh big North Liverpool school engagement, a ladies' dinner. I always expect that people who book me know what I do (this was 2005 by the way) so you can always Google me. It was organised by a woman who was a teacher in a Catholic school.

It was also PTA evening and I thought, 'sorry, love, but you've booked the wrong act.' Especially when I, a Proddy – protestant – was going to do my infamous Pope joke (I'm still not going to tell it in this book – you will have to buy the CD, or come and see me and I will sign the book and write 'Pope Joke').

I was prepared to say to this lady: "I will go home. Here's your money back – but she said, "No". I went to the toilet and looked in the mirror at myself (on reflection, who else was there?) and thought: 'OK, if that's what they want, I will go ahead.'

At dinner a head nun . . . there were plenty more – said 'Grace.' They didn't look like nuns – they must have been undercover, plain-clothes nuns. I sat there thinking: 'What the hell (forgive me) am I doing here?' There was sweat rolling down my legs . . . I think it was sweat. I texted hubby number 3 and he rang back. It was the theme music from Tarzan . . . Don't ask.

It could have been worse – a mobile phone soundtrack from The Exorcist or The Omen. He said very astutely: "Have dinner – then f*** off home."

Well, if I think someone doesn't want me to do it then I won't, but this woman who had booked me kept on having a go. She pestered me during my act to cut certain bits. Well, that's like a red rag to a bull. Contraception . . . amongst other subject matters.

My view was – and is – that people had paid to see me and they WERE going to see and hear me. The end point being, we were, in reality, raising money for charity.

A lot of people loved it. I don't know about the plain- clothes nuns. That teacher didn't. I did about 30 minutes, but I was haunted by it for months afterwards. Even now I break out in a cold sweat (what's that down my legs, again?).

The happy ending is that during that evening a woman came up to me and booked me for a show to raise money for a sick child. I went. I did it. But, oh that ladies' dinner . . . what a disaster. Amen!

Someone once asked me if I get stage fright. Stage fright is something that ruins people like the great impressionist Mike Yarwood, who just couldn't physically do it. The only time I've ever thrown up sick was before the West End, because I knew there was an awful lot riding on it. I did throw up in a bucket, but I never did it again – I was fine after that.

I get a total adrenaline rush and I do get nerves. For instance, if I know I'm doing a gig next week in a place that potentially is all different to me, or it's all men or all snooty golf club people. I'll have started worrying about that two weeks before. So I will get extremely nervous. I pace up and down a lot before I go on.

I find that most singers will go on and do somebody else's songs, and I'm not being detrimental at all to singers. People will then decide if they like that song or they don't. If they like the song they'll clap and cheer – if they don't, they 'll just clap. With a comic it's totally different.

It's you.

It's personal.

You have to, within three minutes or less, establish a rapport with people you've never met before, and they've never met you, and you've got to get them to at least like you at little bit. So that 10 minutes in they'll love you. That's like opening a big zip from your head to your toes, and just saying: "Well, this is me."

And this is all I've got.

And that's the hard part – that's the nervy part.

Everybody's sense of humour is different. If I go to the Midlands, I have to slow down my accent a great deal. If I go to London I have to slow it down. All around the south-east and west coast you have to slow the accent down.

Places like Cardiff and Swansea – you're fine. Most of South Wales in fact, you're fine, and North Wales provides pretty good audiences.

The North East is very much like Liverpool – it's tough, hard, working areas, and if you make them laugh then you deserve your place in life. Glasgow is exactly the same.

Manchester's tough if you've got a Scouse accent, very tough, because they have this immediate shield that comes up if you're a Scouser. Apparently it goes back to the Manchester Ship Canal.

It goes back an awful long way and there is a distinct dislike for a Scouser in Manchester, and I will stand by that. I've never been a lover of working in Blackpool because a lot of acts live and work in Blackpool – and they'll work for peanuts – doing two or three hotels a night. I actually hyperventilate if somebody mentions Blackpool – but I'd love to feel welcome there.

Yorkshire's tough, but once you've got 'em they're yours.

North and Southern Ireland are fantastic, absolutely fantastic. Liverpool's the capital of Ireland, anyway!

I remember going to Scotland years and years ago, and I walked into this club and this fella said: "So you're English, are you?"

I said: "Yes."

He asked where I was from. I said: "Liverpool."

He responded: "That's alright then – so you're not English . . ."

NEWSPAPERS

"I don't read the tabloids.
I once edited the Liverpool ECHO for a day, the newspaper's only female editor. Ok, it was only for a day, but still. It was one of the most eye-opening, amazing days of my whole life. I absolutely loved it. My daughter, Sarah, was working there at the time, so it was great to come out of the Editor's chair having held the news and features conference, and then see my daughter standing there talking to friends and fellow journalists. I looked out of the editor's office and said: "Haven't you got a job to do?"
She replied: "Mother, give me a pay rise."
It must run in the family (cheek).
I love my local papers, though – and always will."

MY HERO –
SIR PAUL McCARTNEY

"I'd like to put Macca on my all time heroes list.
Now, by rights, I should have put him on my
bitter bus because, as a young girl, he broke my
heart. TWICE. First, when he got engaged to actress
Jane Asher. Secondly, when he married American
photographer Linda Eastman, who became the equally
famous Linda McCartney. But, since growing up (sort
of), I have grown to love him in a different way.
He is so very true to Liverpool, and he calls himself the
scruff from Speke. Paul comes and goes without any
fuss and he has helped young people from all over the
world with LIPA, his Liverpool School for Performing
Arts. It was his old Liverpool Institute school, where
Peter Sissons, Mike McCartney and Bill Kenwright went.
Macca has also, with the late Linda's help, provided
us with the Linda McCartney Breast Cancer Centre,
which helps so many women and, of course, this cause
is so dear to my own heart. Husband Number Three
was always jealous. He used to throw stones (not
rolling ones) at him when they were both school kids.
I don't think it's held Macca back ... do you?"

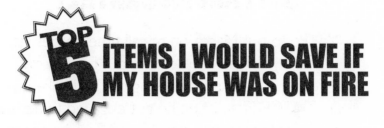

TOP 5 ITEMS I WOULD SAVE IF MY HOUSE WAS ON FIRE

1. MASCARA
I know what you're thinking. The friggin'
house is burning down. But I have
ginger eye-lashes.

2. LULU GUINNESS HANDBAGS
She's got an OBE for doing handbags.
How classy is that? I've got three of her
handbags, and they'd come with me.

3. JEWELLERY BOX
For sentimental value.
Every piece means something and
brings back the memories.

4. FAMILY PHOTO
A picture of me, my mum, dad and Sarah.

5. ONCE UPON A TIME IN AMERICA
A brilliant film I have on DVD.
Robert De Niro at his most handsome.

CHAPTER 14

All the Worlds a Stage

"Who would have thought it?
I always wanted to join the
circus, and now I have."

MEET Pauline Daniels: the Impresario. All the world's a stage. Box office manager, director and star of my own theatre. Who would have thought it? I always wanted to join the circus, and now I have. I set up the Actors' Studio and it's now five-years-old.

I have to apologise for answering the phone during a chat with every budding scriptwriter, artiste or journalist who knocks on the door. "Hello, Actors' Studio," I say. That's it. It's a dream come true.

Once I said: "Tickets for Shirley Valentine . . . yes, I have a few left."

"Sorry NOT for THAT day – it's sold out – has been for weeks." I stubbed out a ciggie and looked out of the window.

"I might have a few returns, though."

It seemed like a sketch, a play within a play, but this is for real. It's my one-woman show and my one-woman theatre. It's all here; a multi-purpose office with couch (not casting), an actor's mirror – all those showbiz bulbs – and an array of grease-paint.

Photos of family, friends and theatrical keepsakes. It was a risk – a gamble – but it's great seeing the enthusiasm in new writers and performers, coming in with the same enthusiasm that I had.

I've never been called an 'impressario' before.

At the Actors' Studio I am theatre manager, box office receptionist, publicity officer, hospitality queen and resident celebrity – but I always put writers and actors first. The building used to be the Liverpool Academy of Arts Exhibition venue, run by neighbour June Lornie, which she moved next door.

I still support every arts venture. When the Academy went and left the space, with the best working cafe in Britain underneath (Sue does the best ever poached eggs), it was something I thought long and hard about being involved with. I was itching to do something with it and I did. So I contacted the landlord and we came to an arrangement.

I went for it and got it.

I put on a few performances of 'Talking Heads', which was a great success, and I knew there were things I could really do here.

I could feel it and I thought: "If you see a chance, take it" – so I did. And I want to do more here.

Seating at first, though, was a real problem. I thought: "What am I going to do?" I want people to be comfortable in the theatre. Then, out of the blue, I heard that the New Brighton Floral Pavilion was being totally refurbished.

I rang the fabulous Paul Holiday, who donated the seats, and he gave me display cabinets for outside the theatre where I can – and still do – pin up posters and print rave reviews. Having those seats is a bit of real theatre history. One theatre passing on a legacy to another. Lovely.

And my actor pal, former Brookside star Neil Caple, built me theatre wings on either side of the stage so we have a real fully-fledged live breathing theatre.

Theatre people do stick together. It was just brick walls before. It's not now. I am glad it has turned into a vibrant venue that is gaining a great reputation, and as somewhere where new work can be put on and where you can feel an intimacy with the people on stage. The run of 'Shirley Valentine' has sold out numerous times. "Last run," I once said. But I never say never.

It is funny when people ring up and book for a show and they don't realise it's ME answering the phone. One caller said: "I believe Pauline Daniels is very good in this production . . . she got 10 out of 10 in reviews."

And I respond: 'Well, that's a pretty good recommendation, madam. But I'm not one to blow my own trumpet!"

Yes I am . . . why not?

Being artistic director, too, I am excited about bringing new works to the venue. It's a theatre that opens its doors to everyone.

A good, old-fashioned pay-on-the-door theatre. I told one lady: "You can't swipe that here, love."

We did a Scouse production called 'Madonna and Me' by Tommy Kearney, which had been a success in London and across the country, but it couldn't get a home in Liverpool – but it had one with me.

I always want to put on a programme of events that is wide-ranging. I looked at a script for a one-woman show, written especially for me, about a washed-up comedienne and a soap star. And – before you ask – it was not biographical. I am also looking at a show featuring four monologues lasting 15 minutes, each called 'Four by Fifteen'.

I am open to persuasion. There is so much talent out there and I know who will make it. New girl writers, new lad writers. Sometimes, someone will always surprise you. I love being able to say 'World Première' on posters. I really love that. I am keen to keep local talent in work. In 'Shirley Valentine', the set and backroom team were from local colleges and universities – I always want to encourage more of that.

I never really liked John Lennon until, in 2010, a young playwright called Scott Murphy came to me with his latest script called 'Walls and Bridges' (named after one of John's albums).

It was about John Lennon's 'lost weekend', when Yoko asked him to leave – a sort of trial separation – and he went on a bit of a bender in Los Angeles with Harry Nilsson. So we put the play on, about John looking back on his life, and it did really well.

After it was over, and for a laugh, we decided to take it to the Brighton Fringe Festival, and with ambitions even higher, we also applied to the New York Fringe.

Guess what? Brighton didn't want to know but New York did. So, as this book was being written the talented cast were in the Big Apple. I had to stay behind and look after the theatre, but I was proud to be the director.

I like directing, and doing that play was another first, because I learned something.

At the same time there was a TV documentary on BBC about John, and it tallied with what we had said. I was never very fond of John Lennon – the man, his bitterness – but I saw him differently from the play's point of view.

Life is full of 'if' – John knew that. He was at his lowest ebb, but John could always laugh and that's what the play brought over. I tried to invite Yoko to see it, when she was on a visit to Liverpool, but her minders slammed the door on that one.

'Walls and Bridges' was John's comment that life is full of walls you walk into, but bridges you can cross.

Maybe Yoko will pop in and see it . . . one day.

While Seel Street is my own base, I am excited about still performing and my own career is going on outside of the theatre. I have toured with Ricky Tomlinson's 'Laughter Show', and continue with my own solo gigs. I take every job very seriously.

In my own theatre it's brilliant because it's all ME along with a few volunteers, and my last hubby who helped a bit – he was a dab hand at ticket-collecting.

I would love to expand one day and get a 150-seater theatre. I was going to call it 36 Seel Street because it tells people where we are. But I like the legacy of the 'Liverpool Academy of Arts'.

Actors' Studio has a nice ring about it, though, doesn't it?

HOW TO FIND THE PERFECT HUSBAND

"Hang around a nursing home and find out which one's got the worst cough and the most dosh."

TOP 5 SHAKESPEARE PLAYS I TURNED DOWN

1. TWELFTH NIGHT

2. ROMEO AND JULIET
The nurse, before you ask.

3. KING LEAR
The Fool – a woman in a man's world again!

4. MIDSUMMER NIGHT'S DREAM
'Bottom'

5. RICHARD III
'The hump'

MY PIRATES OF THE CARIBBEAN – DREAM ROLE

"Captain Jill Sparrow, Johnny Depp's wife . . .
OR Privateer
'Has Anyone Seen My Parrot' Daniels"

CHAPTER 15

She's a Jolly Good Fellow!

"In 2009, John Moores University honoured me with their highest accolade, an Honorary Fellowship. It was, and still is, the best thing that has ever happened to me."

IN 2009 John Moores University honoured me with their highest accolade, an Honorary Fellowship. It was, and still is, the best thing that has ever happened to me.

Flashback to December 2008: I was at my little theatre and I picked up the post from the pigeon hole, and saw JMU on the envelope. I was supposed to be mentoring someone so I never bothered opening it straight away, I just put it on my desk and went downstairs for my breakfast in the cafe.

After one of Sue's bacon butties, I went upstairs to my little office and opened the mail. I couldn't believe the letter I was reading – it was from the vice-chancellor and it was asking me to accept an Honorary Fellowship for my continued contribution to the world of performing arts.

I read it again and again.

I cried again and again.

Me!

Little me!

No it couldn't be! (that rhymes – now I'm a poet 'n' all).

I rang Kenny and he cried. I rang my mum and dad and they cried. I wasn't supposed to tell anyone, but I figured that husbands, parents and kids were okay. I was a bit worried about Sarah because I didn't know how she would take it. She always seemed a bit angry when pop stars and actors and people like that got honorary degrees, but she was thrilled for me.

I then had to keep my mouth shut for as long as it took. I was in the Playhouse one evening at a press night and Roger Phillips, my old mate from Radio Merseyside, said that he wanted to introduce me to someone. It was 'the' Michael Brown, vice-chancellor of JMU. He said to me: "You don't know me but I have been sending you letters and emails since December."

I just hugged him and said: "When can I say something"?

"You can't", was the answer.

That is the hardest thing I have ever had to do, keep my mouth shut. I can't hold my own water usually, but I was really good with this. In May 2009 it went into the local papers and was on local radio, I could now tell the world – and I did.

If I could have stood on the top of the Liver Building and screamed it, I would have.

The night before the ceremony was the dinner. I was a bit scared that everyone would be a bit posh for me, but they were all wonderful. Brian May of Queen was there, he is the chancellor of JMU.

God, he's tall and, sorry Brian, love, but after seeing that head of hair up close and personal (it was like a pile of Shredded Wheat) I was seriously thinking . . . GET SOME PRODUCT.

The next day we picked up mum and dad. Lunch first – we had our own table: me, Kenny, mum, dad, Sarah and her husband Ed, my great friend Chris McCabe and Emma Lisi, my favourite up-and-coming actress.

I was having my robe and cap made for me. I had picked the colours and everything, but I hadn't seen it. After lunch they took my mum and dad to the cathedral to get them settled for the ceremony, and they took me away to be robed. I feel a dickhead telling you this now, but when I tried my gown on I just looked in the mirror and then the floodgates opened. I cried and cried and it took me ages to stop.

I took my place in the procession and calmed myself down. I was so proud, walking the length of the cathedral aisle and when I got to the end, there in the front was my family. I looked at mum and dad and they started crying and then Kenny did too. It was just a whinge-fest.

I took my place on the stage next to Roger Phillips and watched what seemed like thousands of young people getting their degrees, and then it was my turn.

They had asked me to prepare an acceptance speech and keep it to three or four minutes. I couldn't write anything, I had always spoken from the heart and I couldn't do this any differently.

I didn't have any notes, I just got up and spoke. I threw in a few gags and had the Anglican Cathedral rolling in the aisles, and it went really well. I will never forget, to my dying day, the feeling I had and I am so glad that dad was there to see it all.

At the ceremony, Professor Frank Sanderson, Honorable Pro-Chancellor of JMU, read out the following citation:

"I have pleasure in presenting Pauline Daniels for the award of an Honorary Fellowship from Liverpool John Moores University.

"Birkenhead-born Pauline Daniels made her name as Britain's best female stand-up comedian, noted for her spot-on comic timing.

Progressively, she has extended her range as an entertainer to great effect, achieving acclaim as an actress and singer on the stage and on television.

"This consummate performer now finds time through her ownership and management of the Actor's Studio on Seel Street to feature in her own productions and provide great opportunities for emerging local talent.

"She is convinced that no other city has such a concentration of creative talent and has begun running comedy classes from the Studio. She proudly pronounced the Capital of Culture celebrations: 'Look out World, we are on the up. We are brimming with culture, but we have something no other city has ... Scousers'.

"Scousers she describes as, 'friendly, helpful, funny - and bloody good at football'.

"Pauline Daniels was born in Birkenhead in June 1955, the only child of Charles and Doreen.

"After Mersey Park junior school Pauline attended Prenton Park Secondary school in the late 60s, and despite the strict atmosphere she had a happy time there. She does however recall with some satisfaction that the headmistress wrongly predicted, "you'll never get anywhere in life young lady by being a clown".

"Pauline has proved her emphatically wrong, and when she took over the Actor's Studio on Seel Street in 2007, she emphasised the point: 'I always wanted to join the circus and now I have'.

"After leaving school at sixteen, Pauline wanted to be an actress but with no means of supporting herself through theatre school, she bluffed her way into a succession of office jobs, but her bluff was called when she took a job as a telex operator and was put in a room with a telex machine but with no idea as to how the telex machine actually worked.

"Her first experience as an entertainer was in her early 20s as a singer in a Wallasey-based trio. One night, a sore throat restricted her singing and so she told a few jokes to such good effect that jokes became an important part of the act.

"Then came the first of many stage roles - at the Liverpool Playhouse as Mama Morton in 'Chicago' in 1986, followed by Rose in 'Gypsy' at the same venue.

"After a variety of musical, comedy and straight roles, she began her legendary run as Willy Russell's favourite Shirley Valentine in 1992 and has continued to play the definitive Shirley all over the country, recently at her own Actor's Studio.

"Pauline has put her great singing voice to good use, performing with the Liverpool Philharmonic on several occasions and made her West-End debut in 1999, starring as Faye Bogle in the smash-hit musical 'A Saint She Ain't' where she very effectively parodied Mae West – for whom she has a great respect and affection.

"In 2002 she starred with Jo Monro and Sam Kane in the musical comedy 'Women on the Verge of HRT' which she expects will tour in the near future.

"And Pauline's impressive range as an actress was movingly demonstrated in the play 'Unprotected' at the Everyman in 2006 when she played the mother of a murdered Liverpool prostitute, a performance which won her huge plaudits.

"Pauline has made numerous television appearances: she was in Carla Lane's 'Bread' and Phil Redmond's 'Brookside' where she played Maria Benson in a twelve month run.

"And notably, Pauline was the first and only female comic to feature in ITV's 'The Comedians'. She also had a two-year spell co-presenting with Roger Phillips on Radio Merseyside. Roger describes Pauline as: 'always kind, always positive and always great fun', remembering with affection the time they were in the Everyman production of Elsie and Norm's 'Macbeth'.

"Recently, the ever-busy Pauline starred in several productions at her Actor's Studio, including a production of Alan Bennett's 'Talking Heads', and at the Royal Court in 'Dirty Dusting'. She will play the leading role in Helen Forrester's tale of a family fallen on hard times, 'Twopence to Cross the Mersey', when it returns to the Empire this autumn. And then Panto at the Floral Pavillion New Brighton where she will play the Wicked Queen in 'Snow White and the Seven Dwarves'.

"At the Actor's Studio, Pauline is not only the theatre manager, box-office receptionist, artistic director and publicity officer but she also answers the phone. During the sell-out run of 'Shirley Valentine', Pauline picked up the phone and the caller said: "I believe Pauline is very good in it . . . she got ten out of ten in the ECHO". And Pauline, not normally one to blow her own trumpet, replied: "Well, that's a pretty good recommendation, madam."

"Joe Riley describes her as: 'the best ever Shirley

Valentine', Peter Grant marvels at her effortless communication with her audiences, and BBC's Spencer Leigh has applauded her strength as an actress, noting in one production that she transformed herself so well that he felt that another actress had come onto the stage.

"Pauline is frequently involved in raising funds for worthy causes, on several occasions playing Shirley Valentine in aid of charities.

"She has given her support to Age Concern and many local cancer-related charities such as the Lily Centre, Jospice, The Roy Castle Lung Cancer Foundation and The Linda McCartney Centre.

"'Being born on the other side of the water doesn't stop me being proud of this great city of which I have become an adopted daughter and a semi-skilled Scouser,' she says.

"She found 2008, the Capital of Culture Year, fantastic, bringing a buzz to the city she'd never known – despite the event being opened by someone she describes as: "the worst drummer in the world".

Pauline Daniels loves Liverpool and Liverpool loves Pauline Daniels. And today we are delighted to show our appreciation for this true professional, this multi-talented comedienne, actress, and singer for her outstanding and on-going contribution to the performing arts.

"Thus I have great pleasure in presenting Pauline Daniels, this most distinguished adopted daughter of our city, for admission to our highest honour of Fellow of Liverpool John Moores University."

I have only ever had two other awards – well, three actually, but they never felt like they really should be mine, if you know what I mean.

The first goes back to about 1981 when Ernie Mac, who ran the Montrose Club in Liverpool, rang me and asked whether I was available on this particular date. When I told him I was, he said: "Oh well, you've won a Variety Club award!" I can't help thinking that if I hadn't been available then somebody else would have got it.

The next award was a 'Scouseology'. This award has been running for about 20 years and I won it in the early days for the 'Battle of the Sexes' show I did with Tom Pepper, so I don't really feel as though I won that one, either.

The last award I won was a 'Woman of the Year' accolade in 2005. It wasn't even in a category, it was as if the panel had sat around the table and someone had said: "You know, we had better give Pauline Daniels something before she dies."

So that's what they did. I didn't die, though.

Please don't get me wrong – I am grateful for all these awards, but you have to agree that they all pale into insignificance when you find out that you have been awarded an honorary Fellowship from such a great university as John Moores.

I have never done the job I do to win awards. My accolades have been my audiences. They are the ones that show you you're doing things right. They are the ones that really matter but every now and again, if someone wants to say thank you by giving you a token, then that's fantastic. Although I have to say that the spelling on my 'Woman of the Year' award was wrong, and I never noticed for about six months!

It was in pride of place on the coffee table. I cleaned it every week and then one day Kenny said: "Hey, the word 'Merseyside' has got an 's' missing."

From that day on it's in a cabinet. You can see it, but it's angled so that you can't read the bloody thing. So, you see, I'm sure you can understand how important it is.

In 2007 it was Liverpool's 800th birthday and the Liverpool Echo published a special pull-out which hailed the best 800 Merseysiders ever and there I was – now that's really something I am proud of too.

If I ever get Doctor or Professor, I could get an upgrade on a plane then. Okay, I couldn't write prescriptions and I wouldn't want to examine anyone's piles – but it would be nice to be Doctor Daniels.

I love the graduation picture of mum, dad, Ken and me. It's by my bedside. Dad looked great, I don't half miss him. I've still got the gown, it's at home. I've always fancied going to Tesco in it.

I have been used as an exhibit in the new Museum of Liverpool as well. I have done a CD of my life and you will be able to go and press a picture of me and I'll talk to you.

Tony Brown, a brilliant artist captured me – in 2008, Liverpool's Capital of Culture year. He was putting together a 'One Hundred Heads' exhibition, featuring 100 people who had been influential on Merseyside.

I was one of those heads. He took my photo and then

with photographs and press cuttings he made up my face, a bit like a mosaic – a collage – but a million times better. Please try and see it – I am sure it winks back.

BIGGEST WEAKNESSES

"My biggest weaknesses are
GETTING MARRIED,
CHAMPAGNE and CHINESE FOOD"

BIGGEST IMPULSE BUY

"A £600 silk jacket.
It looked like an anorak. Dave just
looked at me and said: 'You paid
£600 for a f***ing anorak'."

MOTTOS

"I believe you make your own luck. It doesn't find you — you have to work hard for everything. If you don't, you'll never appreciate anything. And my motto? Treat other people as you would like to be treated yourself."

CHAPTER 16

And in The End

"Here's to the next part of my life, time for me to stand up and be counted."

WE lost my dad, "Little Big Man", on February 24, 2010.

I realised that although I have had many boyfriends and three husbands I had never, until that time, had my heart broken. I feel empty but I know I have to be strong for mum and Sarah. When the vicar came round to discuss the finer details of the service and so on, we all cheered up because he was fantastic. He was as mad as a box of frogs but we loved him.

We knew that the funeral would be a great celebration and it was. I scraped up every bit of bravery I had and did the tribute to my dad. No one else knew him like we did, and mum and Sarah couldn't have done it on their own. I know Copper would have been made up, the chapel was full and because of the little stories I told about him, it rang out with laughter. We left the chapel to Perry Como singing 'Magic Moments'.

We chose that for three reasons: Perry was one of dad's favourites, and we had had so many magic moments with him. But the main reason, and one nobody else but our little family knew, was that Copper used to sing rude words to it. Google it to hear the melody then singalong, starting with:

"*Remember the night you fell in the s****,*
With your best suit on,
The suit that you got, from saving a lot
Of Embassy coupons . . ."
Magic moments.

God Bless Dad. Night night. x x x

My life has been full of twists and turns and can change with just one phone call. You never know where that can take you and, in a way, that's allowed.

Life will always hold surprises for you.

I moved out of my third marital home as this book was being written. Now, how's that for a surprise? Husband Number Three has gone, but it seems par for the course for me, doesn't it, girls?

I really thought that this one, was THE ONE.

Still, it's onwards and upwards. And when that phone call does come, I won't have to worry about where it takes me now.

I hope that in this book, you've enjoyed the highs, felt a little for me during the lows, and I really hope that, along the way, you laughed a great deal. You can always come up and see me sometime . . .

So, here's to the next part of my life. Time for me to stand up and be counted.

Isn't that right . . . dear, dear wall?

THE PAULINE DANIELS GUIDE ON HOW TO...

ENJOY YOUR HEN NIGHT
Talk the bride out of it. Then get hammered.

KEEP YOUR SEX LIFE HOT
Set fire to the curtains in the bedroom.

COOK
Stay out of the kitchen. If you are anything like me when it comes to culinary art, you just might kill someone.
I asked my fella once where we should go on holiday.
I said: "I'd like to go somewhere different."
He said: "Try the bloody kitchen".

LOOK AFTER YOUR PURSE
Never worry about the money you owe. After all, YOU owe it. Let the bastards you owe it to worry about whether they'll ever get it.

STAY YOUNG LOOKING
Don't trick yourself into thinking that a facelift is the answer. I raised my own eyebrows.
When I've seen all the famous faces around, who have had so much work on them, they look false.
Anne Robinson no longer has any expressions left.
Joan Rivers looks almost Chinese and Cilla has had that many, she could wear her arse for a hat.

KEEP LOVE ALIVE

When your marriage turns into that magical friendship, spend more time laughing together than arguing and crying. Although a good row, now and again, is very healthy. Just don't let the bad feelings linger.

LOOK AFTER YOUR BODY

Look after your health. I recently had a colonoscopy. For all the good that was, you might as well have shoved it up my arse!

The sad thing was they wouldn't give me the photos they took – now that would freak the kids out if I put one of those on Facebook as a profile picture.

And finally . . .

GO TO YOUR GRAVE HAPPY

Live to forgive . . . but never forget.

Lie about being dead, throw a big celebration party and then turn up in disguise to see who shows up to fill their faces. No, I'm only joking. Love and treasure your mum, dad and kids. Be as true to yourself as you possibly can without hurting anybody.

And if you haven't got any money to give to someone who needs it, then give them your time.

Take a Bow

SO there you have it – it's official. Pauline Daniels is an inspiration. A fighter – a winner.

An award-winning stand-up. One moment in her company and you will see why she can spend hours on stage telling stories, going off on tangents, but always getting back to her original point, the art of every great comic.

She loves to make people laugh and she is proud to be one of the most respected women in her profession.

So here, we present some tributes to Pauline.

Pauline: Hey, I'm not dead yet!

Ed: Shut up and listen. This is what your fellow performers think about you . . .

PETER GRANT
Book Editor

WILLY RUSSELL
Play writer

Pauline is a unique Shirley Valentine. As a performer, what she has done is great, because so few women have cracked that gig over a lifetime.

There is NO definitive Shirley Valentine. But Pauline is unique in that she brought – and brings – three factors to her interpretation.

1) She is Liverpudlian
2) A stand-up comedienne
3) A great versatile actress

Question: Did I have any initial doubts about casting her as Shirley? Yes. Could she do the seriousness? Yes.

She has been in shows with me and Alan Bleasdale before, notably with our 'Crazy Nights' at the Playhouse.

Pauline has been in 'Breezeblock Park' and she has been in the revamped 'Our Day Out' at the Royal Court.

She is special. She has quality.

Pauline Daniels is OUR LADY OF PERPETUAL COMEDY.

SAM AVERY
Award-Winning Comedian, Royal Court

Pauline was a huge inspiration for female comics, and caused a lot of perspiration for male comics.

When she came along, girls realised they, too, could get on the stage, and the blokes knew that it wasn't a closed shop anymore.

PETE PRICE
Award-Winning Broadcaster

Pauline does a fantastic line in panto (oh, yes she does) as the Wicked Queen.

When I have been appearing with her, I would creep up and then the kids would shout: "He's behind you!"

She would, with perfect timing, say without flinching or looking around . . . ice cool:

"It's alright, I'm, not worried about HIM."

Pauline Daniels is someone I knew before she was famous, before she was rightly recognised as an accomplished stand-up comedienne and stage and TV personality.

She is a powerful comic – first and foremost – but with a great voice.

She is also very sensitive.

Sometimes I think that hard veneer is a facade – the professional on stage and the vulnerable off it.

I have to say, she scared the men when she did her formidable showcase, 'The Battle of the Sexes'.

It is a tall order to keep a balance in the club, theatre and stand-up world but she has done it and continues to do it.

One word sums her up, in my view, and it begins with a T. (Stop that – this isn't a panto).

It's T for 'Tremendous.' Pauline, look behind you.

Oh, please yourself, it's only me.

PS. Pauline, can you mention my autobiography 'Namedropper', available in all good book shops. I'm available for signing sessions . . .

ROGER PHILLIPS
Sony Gold Award Winning BBC Broadcaster

Pauline Daniels is one of those people you never forget.

I'd known her a bit before working with her for two years on the mid-morning show at BBC Radio Merseyside.

I'd always admired her as a stand-up comedian. She breaks all the barriers and more.

And above all, she makes you roar with laughter at her particular view of life – and womens' lives in particular.

Could she do the same on radio?

Of course she did. She was an absolute treasure to work with – and 'with' is the right word.

She was a really generous co-presenter, allowing me just enough space to hang myself!

She's so quick responding to callers. So knowledgeable about music. And she comes across on the microphone just as she is – a really loveable person.

As an actress, she's outstanding – the very best Shirley Valentine I've ever seen.

She's also a skilled theatre director and I've had the privilege of being directed by her, as well as watching her productions.

Perhaps the highlight of our relationship was when we appeared together in the two-hander 'Elsie and Norm's Macbeth'.

We had a ball. Despite the fact that I tried (unsuccessfully) to nick all her jokes through the run.

Long may she continue to entertain us all.

STAND UP & BE COUNTED

NEIL FITZMAURICE
Film Producer, Screenwriter, Stand-up comedian and
Co-writer of 'Phoenix Nights'

She's a bitch. No. I love her to bits. I do. I owe her for the early breaks she gave me.

I was in a big talent show and they were looking for an up-and-coming comedian and she was on the prestigious judging panel. She voted for me and I won.

Then she had her own radio show and asked me to review the news and the papers.

In later life, I was producing one of my films 'Charlie Noades, RIP' and I had her play my mum.

Pauline is very lovely with a great voice and a versatility that I didn't realise she had.

What a great actress she is.

CHARLIE LANDSBOROUGH
Multi-award Winning Recording Star and Singer-Songwriter

I call her 'Our Pauline'.

It's not like work being on stage with her.

We are both comics who act, so we have served the same apprenticeship. She's a fighter and survivor and an inspiration. When you are in a show with her you know she gives 100 per cent and she is a team player.

A great actress and all-rounder.

But she's a star, Our Pauline.

RICKY TOMLINSON
Actor, King of the Royle Family, Singer-songwriter, Author,
Club Owner of the Green Room, Liverpool
(That's enough free credits now.)

She is the ultimate professional. When you hear her song 'Pearl's A Singer' – wow!

I've worked with her on our 'Ricky Tomlinson's Laughter Show' (good, I am glad I can put a plug in there). She is always on time. She's impeccable and she just knows, instinctively, who her audience is.

We have never fallen out. Amazing when you think the show we all do. She is established. No one, but no one, gives men stick like her. (Not even my Rita).

Another great thing about Pauline is that she has always got it in her mind to get IT right. She goes out there and does it. Pauline, for me, always gets it right.

MICKY FINN
Comedian and Actor

She is like me without the moustache. I admire her because being in a play with her, or in a panto, she is one of the lads. She is great, girls.

Just look at her CV – television, West End, Palladium and now she runs her own theatre.

It doesn't get much better when Ken Dodd writes the foreword for her life story and Willy Russell closes it.

(Not the career but the book.)

Pauline, you have always said: "Stand up and be counted". Good on yer, girl.

MARK MORAGHAN
Actor, Crooner and Singer-Songwriter

Pauline is the ultimate professional. Brilliant actress, singer, comic. Brilliant friend. We have worked together in different shows such as 'Twopence to Cross The Mersey', 'Our Day Out' and 'You'll Never walk Alone'.

She really is a ballsy performer – a feisty woman who broke into a world dominated by men and is still going strong and getting stronger. I love working with her and will hopefully, again and again, given the chance.

An inspiring woman.

SAM KANE
Television and Stage Star

Pauline is the only person I know, that after talking to her for five minutes, I have to use my asthma inhaler because I've laughed myself into full respiratory attack.

I can honestly say that she is one of the most genuine and lovely people I've ever met. For me, Pauline's humility is her biggest talent. The generosity she gives as a comedian and actress, and most of all as a human being, is gorgeous. She has the knack of making you feel like you've known her forever as a close friend.

That's a special gift. When it's all over, it would be lovely to be recognised and acclaimed for our achievements. I have no doubt that Pauline will be. Most of all, in my opinion, it would be our greatest accolade to be remembered as a good and lovely person. Pauline Daniels is all of the above. I adore her! She's just ace.

244

ROB FENNAH
Alternative Radio, Producer and Screenwriter

It wasn't until the mid-1990s that I got the chance to work with Pauline for any length of time.

I had just written 'Twopence to Cross the Mersey' (based on Helen Forrester's best-selling book) and I needed a comic actress to play the part of Mrs Foster, a fiery streetwise landlady who screwed the hapless Forrester family for every penny they had.

Pauline played the role perfectly and I didn't hesitate in asking her back when the show was restaged.

I thought Pauline would jump at the chance but to my surprise she refused. "I'll only appear in Twopence again if you give ME the leading role", she replied, bold as brass. "What?" I gasped, somewhat taken aback, "You want to play Helen Forrester, a role that requires one to speak with a really, really posh English accent?"

"You 'eard", Pauline fired back, "give me the lead role and I guarantee you won't regret it".

I did – and I didn't. Pauline followed in the footsteps of Eleanor Bron and Liz Robertson who had played Helen Forrester in previous productions and, despite my worries about the posh accent,

Pauline pulled it off better than I could have ever expected. She has since made the role her own.

Hats off to you, Pauline.

You're a brilliant actress, a great singer, wonderful comedienne and, most important of all, a top mate.

Your recognition as one of the UK's finest entertainers is well deserved.

My Life in Showbiz

"Star of stage, screen
and stand-up"

FIRST PERFORMANCE

I started doing clubs in the back end of 1979.
Yeah, that was the start of it . . .

STAGE

1986	**CHICAGO** – (Mama Morton) Liverpool Playhouse
1987	**COMEDIANS** – (McBrain) Liverpool Everyman – all female version
1988	**GYPSY** – (Rose) Liverpool Playhouse
1991	**SHIRLEY VALENTINE** – National Tour
1994	**TWOPENCE TO CROSS THE MERSEY** – (Mrs Foster) Liverpool Empire
1996	**BILLY LIAR** – Liverpool Playhouse
1997	**SHIRLEY VALENTINE** (lead) – Bill Kenwright, Liverpool Playhouse
1998	**ELSIE AND NORM'S MACBETH** – (Elsie) Liverpool Everyman
1999	**A SAINT SHE AINT** – King's Head / Apollo Theatre
2001	**OLIVER TWIST** – (Mrs Sowberry / Widow Corney) Liverpool Playhouse
2002	**WOMEN ON THE VERGE OF HRT** Mrs McClure, Belgrade Theatre Coventry
2003	**BREEZEBLOCK PARK** – (Betty) Liverpool Playhouse
2005	**SNOW WHITE** – (Wicked Queen)
2005	**MISERY** – (Annie) Brindley Theatre, Runcorn
2005	**AND THE BEAT GOES ON** – (Main artiste) Liverpool Everyman
2006	**UNPROTECTED** – (Pat / Jill) Liverpool / Edinburgh

2006	TALKING HEADS – A Cream Cracker Under the Settee – (Lady of Letters) Tour
2006	CINDERELLA – (Baroness Hardup) New Brighton, Floral Pavillion
2007	TWOPENCE TO CROSS THE MERSEY – Liverpool Empire
2007	SHIRLEY VALENTINE – (Actors' Studio)
2008	THE LIFE AND TIMES OF HYLDA BAKER – (Lead) Actor's Studio
2009	DIRTY DUSTING – (Elsie) Royal Court , Liverpool
2009	SHIRLEY VALENTINE – Royal Court, Liverpool
2009	TWOPENCE TO CROSS THE MERSEY – (older Helen Forrester) Liverpool Empire
2010	OUR DAY OUT – (Mrs Kay) Royal Court, Liverpool

TELEVISION

1982	BOYS FROM THE BLACKSTUFF – (Mourner)
1983	SCRAMBLE – (Herself)
1985	WOGAN – (Herself)
1985	THE COMEDIANS – (Herself)
1986	MIKE REID MATES AND MUSIC – (Herself)
1987	THE TOM O'CONNOR ROAD SHOW – (Herself)
1987	SATURDAY ROYAL – (Herself)
1991	THE COMEDIANS – (Herself)
1991	BROOKSIDE – (Maria Benson)
1998	LIVERPOOL 1 – (Mrs Frank)
2007	THE STREET – (Effing Nellie)
2009	BLUE MURDER – (Mrs Hillard)
2010	DOA – (Clive's Wife)

RADIO

1996 | BBC Radio Merseyside Morning,
       Breakfast Show
2008 | Late Nite Show BBC Radio Merseyside

FILM

2008 | CHARLIE NOADES RIP – (Patricia)

ALL OF THE ABOVE
ON-GOING.
STAND UP COMEDY? YOU BET.
COMING SOON TO A TOWN NEAR YOU . . .

Thanks a Million

"You've been such
a lovely audience,
I'd like to take you
home with me . . ."

THANKS to home, my family, Birkenhead for bearing me. Liverpool for nurturing me.

Work experience, Butlin's, ten fabulous years of work and an education in life.

My first agent Ricky McCabe for giving me my first chance – for believing in me and being a good friend along with his lovely family.

Allan Johnstone – the man who KNEW I could open a theatre.

Inspirers, Peggy O'Brien. Winnie Keating. Founders of the Lily Centre Breast Cancer Support Group for showing me what charity really is.

Comedian, Barry Cryer, for teaching me a masterclass in comedy.

Playwright, Willy Russell, for writing for real women and letting me play three of them so far.

Actor and director, Neil Caple, for helping build my flats at the Studio. (The wings, darling.) Oh and for being a mate.

TV star and actor, Michael Starke for making me laugh year after year after year.

Photographer, Jim Connolly. What a photographer. He took the cover shot of this book and a huge version will stand in my Studio. Jim's a lovely, talented man. What a cracker.

Artist and musician, Anthony Brown for creating my life in a piece of art and making me one of his famous 100 Heads touring exhibition. I am now on a wall at the New Brighton Floral Pavilion (isn't that right wall?)

Ed Chapman, my son-in-law, for being a fabulous artist and looking after my little girl.

Kerry my hairdresser. "Who the f***ing hell cuts your hair?"

Johnny Hamp, legendary producer, for having the balls to put a woman on 'The Comedians'. He took a risk but it paid off.

Comedian, Stan Boardman. The only comic who didn't put the knife in my back while making 'The Comedians'.

Director, Ian Kellgren, for giving me the theatre bug and having faith in me throughout the years.

Academic, Michael Brown, retired Vice Chancellor of John Moores University. Nearly 40 years after leaving school, I get the best accolade of my life – a fellowship.

Broadcaster, Ev Draper for giving me the chance to make wavelengths in radio.

Actor and radio star, Roger Philips. He was my right arm when I worked at the BBC and performing with him was always a joy.

Radio legend, Pete Price. Queen of Gossip and one of my best mates.

Thanks to catering – Sue and all at the Cafe at 36 Seel Street. Great tea, banter and butties. Best entertainment show around for me.

Claire Bowles, actress and singer, for being a true friend and having two completely mad sisters.

People. They know who they are.

The club-going population of Merseyside for taking me to their hearts and teaching me what an honest audience is really like.

The Pope, for providing the best joke in my career. Bless him. And I'm not even a Catholic!

I'm still not telling you that joke, so don't ask. You will have to come and see me at one of my shows.

Peter Grant, my Book Editor, and all the talented team at Trinity Mirror.

Husbands.

Number One:

For helping me start on the road.

Number Two:

For giving me an escape route.

Number Three:

For taking me further along the journey to the crossroads. Now I'm thumbing a lift.

Classic comediennes, Phyllis Diller, Joan Rivers and Hylda Baker, for making me realise that women can be funny.

Last and far from least, a fanfare for the King of Comedy, Ken Dodd. When you have loved and admired someone from childhood and they become a fan and a friend, you know that you really are doing OK.

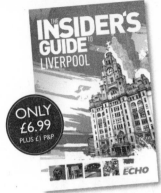
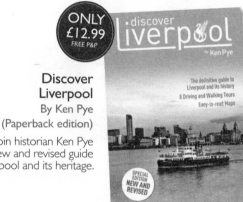

TrinityMirror Media